Soundtracks

Real-life Listening: A Variety of
Subjects, Styles and Speakers

Susan Axbey

Longman

Addison Wesley Longman Limited,
Edinburgh Gate, Harlow,
Essex CM20 2JE, England
and Associated Companies throughout the world.

First published 1989
Fifth impression 1996

Set in 9/10 $\frac{1}{2}$ pt Versailles Roman

Produced by Longman Singapore Publishers (Pte) Ltd
Printed in Singapore

ISBN 0 582 01853 6

Illustrations

Cover illustrated by Diane Fisher

Illustrated by Amy Burch, Chris Burke
Hardlines, Andrew Harris, Andrew Oliver

Acknowledgements

The author and publishers would like to thank all those
people whose voices are heard on the *Soundtracks*
cassette. Our thanks also to reporters, Janey Gordon
for Unit 4 Looking Back and Chris Hawksworth for
Unit 14 The Maniac Mile, and to dramatist, Michael
Richmond for Unit 3 Before Breakfast and Unit 8 The
Macbeth Ordeal.

We are grateful to the following for permission to
reproduce illustrative material in this book:

Mathew Boyle for page 10 (left); Camera Press Limited
for pages 17, 50 (left) and 69 (right); J. Allan Cash
Photolibrary for page 33; Clive Barda
Photography/Harrison/Parrott Limited for page 30;
Friends of the Earth for page 66 (left); The Hulton
Picture Company for page 22 (left); Longman
Photographic Unit for pages 45 and 54; Mark
Boulton/ICCE for page 66 (right); Sub-4/Terry
Lyons/Valley News Pictures for page 65; Topham
Picture Library for pages 22 (right) and 50 (right).

Photographs on pages 10 (right), 14, 26, 46 and 69 (left)
by St John Pope and on pages 34, 42 and 58 by Monica
Wells.

CONTENTS

CONTENTS

INTRODUCTION FOR STUDENTS AND TEACHERS

Who is Soundtracks for?

Soundtracks is intended for students who have studied English for a number of years and reached a good general standard but who need further opportunities to listen to the spoken language. It will be particularly useful for students preparing for the Listening Test of the University of Cambridge First Certificate and Proficiency examinations in English.

Soundtracks can be used in the classroom with a teacher, in a language laboratory or by students working alone.

What are the aims?

The two main aims are:
- to provide students with a wide variety of interesting and authentic listening material
- to practise and improve listening skills through a range of exercises and activities.

Soundtracks also provides follow up oral and written work and opportunities for language study.

What kinds of listening material are included?

The book is accompanied by one C90 cassette. There are fifteen Units of listening each of which is between four and seven minutes long.

These cover a wide variety of material ranging from public announcements to private conversations and from drama to documentary. The speakers come from all walks of life and vary in age and accent. The Map of the book on pages 8–9 gives more information about the range of listening material included.

What is the general approach to listening?

Successful listening in the classroom depends partly on good preparation. It is important for the student to know something about the context of what he or she is going to listen to, i.e. who is speaking, where, when and to what purpose. This kind of information makes it possible to make predictions before and during listening. These may be predictions of content and language. At the same time, students can draw on their own knowledge of the topic or experience of similar situations.

Initial listening tasks should have a general or global understanding as their aim and the material should be listened to from beginning to end without stopping the tape. Appropriate exercises for this first stage of listening are those which promote skills such as:
- listening for gist (general meaning)
- confirming/checking predictions
- understanding key points
- recognising different speakers
- understanding text organisation
- awareness of a speaker's attitude or intention.

For successful listening of this kind, it is not necessary to understand every word or detail of what is being said.

The first kind of listening outlined above can be described as 'natural' in the sense that it tries to mirror the way in which a native speaker might listen to the same material. However, language students are often required, particularly in examinations, to show a more detailed understanding and recall of the material as well. For this type of listening it may be necessary to stop the tape at certain points or to replay parts of it several times. In this case, the kinds of skills which are necessary will include:

- listening for specific information
- listening and note-taking
- remembering vocabulary
- guessing unfamiliar vocabulary
- comprehension of detail
- awareness of grammar and idiom.

Other more 'natural' listening activities are those which allow the student to make a personal response. These include:

- giving a reaction
- giving an opinion
- evaluating what is said.

Further activities such as discussion, talks, interviews and role play encourage students to develop and extend the topic.

A subsidiary role of listening materials is to provide students with a valuable source of data which can be used to learn new vocabulary or to study aspects of grammar or style.

This approach to listening is reflected in the Unit organisation.

How is each Unit organised?

Each Unit has six sections:

- *Pre-listening*
  This prepares students for the language and content of the listening material.
- *Extensive listening*
  Students aim to achieve a general or global understanding of the material and do not need to understand every word or detail.
- *Intensive listening*
  A more detailed understanding of specific points is required to do these exercises.
- *Follow-up*
  A variety of oral activities encourages discussion and a personal response to what has been heard.
- *Study point*
  This section deals with particular language points arising from the listening material. The focus may be on grammar, function, vocabulary or style.
- *Writing*
  Students are given practice in the different kinds of writing they are expected to be able to produce at this level.

What types of listening exercises are there?

There is a wide range of exercise types in the *Extensive and Intensive listening* sections which includes the following:

counting	note-taking	gap-filling
ordering	completing notes	word completion
matching	multiple choice	sentence completion
selecting	true or false	transcribing
labelling	written answers	

Some of these exercises have visual support in the form of illustrations, diagrams, charts and plans.

How should Soundtracks be used?

- *Unit order*
  The Units are ordered in a way which gives plenty of variety of listening as students work through the book. The more difficult Units come towards the end of the book. However, students and teachers can do the Units in any order they choose.

- *Listening exercises*
  Students should always read the exercises carefully before listening to the tape. For *Extensive listening*, the tape should be played through to the end of the Unit without stopping. For *Intensive listening*, students may wish to replay parts of the tape or to stop the tape at different points while they are doing these exercises. Students doing the listening exercises in a language laboratory have the advantage of being able to work at their own pace.

  Some people will find it necessary and/or interesting to listen to a Unit several times. Others will not. However, students who are preparing for the University of Cambridge examinations in English should remember that in the Listening Test for First Certificate and Proficiency they will hear each section of the listening material twice and will be given time between the sections to read and answer the questions.

- *Study point*
  It is sometimes necessary to look at the tapescript or listen to parts of the tape again in order to do some of these exercises.

- *Answer key*
  Teachers are advised to read through the *Answer key* and the accompanying notes for each Unit before the lesson.

- *Classroom use*
  Each Unit of *Soundtracks* is designed to provide teachers with material for one listening-based lesson lasting an hour or an hour and a half. This would leave the *Study point* and the *Writing* sections to be done on another occasion or to be given as homework when appropriate. However, some teachers may wish to spend longer on the *Follow-up* or to allow students to work cooperatively on the *Study point* and *Writing* sections in the class.

  NB The *Study point* section sometimes focusses on language which can be used in the *Follow-up*. In this case, teachers and students may prefer to work through the *Study point* section before doing the *Follow-up*.

- *Self study*
  Students working alone should read the *Pre-listening* section carefully. Even though it is not possible to talk to another person, it is important to think about the questions as this is a good preparation for the listening. The answers to the *Extensive and Intensive listening* and to the *Study point* exercises are in the *Answer key* at the end of this book together with some explanatory notes. If you are working alone, you cannot do all of the *Follow-up* exercises as these are mainly oral but you may find it interesting to read and think about these sections. You can do the *Writing* if you can find someone to correct and comment on your work.

- *Tapescripts*
  The tapescript for each Unit is given towards the end of this book. Some students may find it useful to listen to the tape and follow the tapescript at the same time. However, students are advised *not* to look at the tapescript until they have worked through the Unit as thoroughly as they can.

MAP OF THE BOOK

UNIT	LISTENING TEXT	STUDY POINT	WRITING TASK
1 An American in London	Interview	a) Making comparisons and contrasts b) Giving opinions	Informal letter
A student gives his impressions of London.			
2 Visiting India	Conversation	a) Informal conversation b) Advice and recommendation	Information guide
Three friends talk about their holidays.			
3 Before Breakfast	Drama	a) Formal and informal style b) Idioms and colloquial language	Dialogue
A young man and woman meet on a train.			
4 Looking Back	Reminiscence	a) Habitual Past b) Non-standard forms	Description and narrative
Three people recall their memories of childhood.			
5 The Long Essay	Tutorial	a) Making suggestions b) Prefixes c) Foreign plurals	Essay plan
A postgraduate student meets her tutor.			
6 A Sense of Humour	Jokes and stories	a) Relative clauses b) Direct and indirect speech	Review
A Scot talks about the British sense of humour.			
7 A Card Trick	Instructions	a) Giving instructions b) Understanding reference	Instructions
A magician explains how to do a card trick.			

UNIT	LISTENING TEXT	STUDY POINT	WRITING TASK
8 The Macbeth Ordeal	Narrative	a) Connectives b) Past Perfect	Narrative
An actor tells a story of bad luck.			
9 Office Life	Telephone conversations	a) Speaking on the telephone b) Business vocabulary	Messages
These secretaries spend much of their time on the phone.			
10 The Exhibition	Public announcements Sales talks	a) Persuasion b) Vocabulary sets	Advertisements
Thousands of people visit the Ideal Home Exhibition every year.			
11 The News	News broadcast	a) The Passive b) Style and vocabulary	News reports
This broadcast includes world news and news about the UK.			
12 Sing Jazz	Opinion and comment	a) Word formation b) Fillers	Short essays
These jazz singers talk enthusiastically about their kind of music.			
13 On the Agenda	Meeting	a) Agreement and disagreement b) Reporting a meeting	Minutes
Polytechnic students hold a meeting of the Film Club Committee.			
14 The Maniac Mile	Commentary Interview	a) Using idioms b) Word formation	An article
This very unusual race is held in Yorkshire every year.			
15 Acid Rain	Lecture	a) Lecture organisation b) Abbreviations	Lecture notes
An expert on pollution talks about the dangers of acid rain.			

An American in London

Mathew is an American student from Boston who is spending a year at a college in London.

Pre-listening

1 Thinking about what you know

a) Americans say 'cookie' when the British say 'biscuit'. When the British say 'lorry', Americans say 'truck'. Can you think of any other examples of the differences between British and American English?

b) Can you tell the difference between a British and an American accent? How would a British and an American person say these words: 'black, all, John'?

2 Predicting content

Apart from the language, what other things do you think an American in London might find strange?

Extensive listening

1 Understanding attitude

a) Which of these statements do you think best sums up Mathew's attitude to Britain?
   i)   He has a generally negative view of Britain and the British.
   ii) He is interested in getting to know Britain.
   iii) He is not happy in Britain.

b) What impression do you have of Mathew? Which of these words do you think describe him?

polite		intolerant		aggressive		depressed	
nervous		frank		cheerful		thoughtful	
shy		friendly		hypocritical		relaxed	

Intensive listening

1 Remembering examples

a) Complete the chart with the examples Mathew gives of the differences between British and American English.

British English	American English
queue	
chips	
	potato chips

b) What are the two expressions he has heard in London which you don't hear in America?

2 Listening for specific details

Choose the picture which best illustrates what Mathew has noticed about young people's appearance in Britain.

a)

b)

c)

3 Note-taking

Complete the notes in the chart below. Write one word only in each gap.

	Britain	USA
young people	• more [1]_____ in politics	• not as much
young people's knowledge of other countries	• more politically [2]_____ • know all about the US and how it's [3]_____	• just have a [4]_____ understanding of a few other countries
reasons (mainly because of the [5]_____)	• hear a lot about America • US policies [6]_____ Britain	• don't hear as much about [7]_____ • Britain's policies [8]_____ affect USA as much

Follow-up

1 Asking questions

Mathew was asked about:

a) the things he found most strange when he first arrived in Britain
b) difficulties with the language
c) young people

He was also asked:

d) to give examples
e) to give his reasons

Write the five questions he was asked. You need not use exactly the same words as the interviewer, but your questions should be polite.

Now, in pairs, write three more questions you would like to ask Mathew about Britain.

Read your questions to the class. Can anyone answer your questions or suggest how Mathew might answer them?

2 Interviewing other students

Find out which students in the class have visited Britain, the USA or another foreign country and decide who you would like to interview.

Prepare six questions to ask this person about the foreign country.

Now carry out the interview in pairs or groups.

Tell the class about the student's impressions and opinions of the country.

Study point

1 Making comparisons and contrasts

These are some of the things Mathew said when he was comparing Britain and the USA.

I never heard the word queue before.
I do notice some differences in the young people.
They seem to be much more radical than the young people in the United States.
Radical, I think, in politics too whereas in America you don't find that much.
You don't hear as much about Britain in America as you hear about the US here.

Now rewrite the sentences below using the word or phrase in brackets. Look at the sentences above to help you.

a) The men wear earrings but you don't see that in my country as much.
   (. . . never . . . so many men . . . before)
b) Of course, the language is mostly very similar.
   (. . . few differences . . .)
c) Young people's clothes in America are very colourful compared to those in London.
   (. . . much more . . . than . . .)
d) There is a lot about the United States in the British press but in American newspapers you see very little about Britain.
   (. . . whereas . . .) (. . . not . . . that much . . .)
e) Young people in Britain seem to be much more politically aware than young people in the United States.
   (. . . not as . . . as . . .)

2 Giving opinions

Mathew used the phrases below when he was giving his opinions about Britain.

Complete the answers to these questions by giving your own opinions.

a) Would you say that British people are more or less reserved than Americans?
Well, I'd say _____

b) Do you think young people in your country are more or less politically aware than their parents' generation?
I think they seem to be _____

c) Why do you think that is?
I think the reason is that _____

d) What kind of clothes do you like wearing best?
I like _____ That's just my own preference.

e) Which would you prefer to visit – Britain or America?
I'd rather _____

Writing

A letter

Imagine you are living in a foreign country or in a different part of your own country.

Write a letter to a friend telling them:
* where you are
* what you have found most strange
* what difficulties you have had, if any
* what you like and dislike about the place and the people

Visiting India

Liz (*right*) is planning a visit to India. She is looking at some photographs taken by her neighbours, Julia (*left*) and Marsha (*centre*), who have both been there on holiday.

Pre-listening

1 Thinking about what you know

a) What do you know about the history and geography of India? Can you give three facts?
b) Do you know where Kashmir is?
c) What is Indian food like? Have you ever tried it?
d) What kind of things do you think visitors to India buy there to take home with them?

2 Expressing your preferences

If you had the chance to visit India, what would you most like to see and do there?

Extensive listening

1 Listening for the main points

Which of these aspects of visiting India come up in the conversation?

food		weather		clothes		things to buy	
guidebooks		sightseeing		transport		cost	

2 Checking comprehension

Are these statements true or false?
a) Julia and Marsha went to India together.
b) They went to the same part of India.
c) The food in Kashmir is very hot.
d) Julia and Marsha liked the food, especially the vegetables.
e) They both enjoyed visiting the gardens.
f) There were not many things they wanted to buy.

Intensive listening

1 Listening for specific information

Choose the correct word or phrase to complete these sentences.

a) Srinagar is
  i) on the plain.
  ii) in the hills.

b) Srinagar is
  i) hotter
  ii) cooler
  than Delhi.

c) Marsha had
  i) pumpkin
  ii) spinach
  in yoghurt sauce.

d) They grow
  i) many vegetables
  ii) mainly spinach
  in Kashmir.

2 Guessing unfamiliar vocabulary

Think about the way you understand these words: '*pack, nest, foot, world*'. Now listen to what Julia said about sightseeing trips and choose the correct meaning of the words below.

We packed the four days with trips.

a) '*packed*' means   i) organised ii) filled iii) listed

We went to Pahalgam . . . just a little mountain town nestling in the foot of the Himalayas.

b) '*nestling*' means   i) sheltering ii) disappearing iii) being built

c) '*foot*' means   i) top ii) bottom iii) back

The scenery was just out of this world.

d) '*out of this world*' means   i) wonderful ii) unusually bad iii) strange

3 Note-taking

Complete the notes. Write only one or two words for each item.

a) **Marsha's bedspread**	b) **wood carvings**	c) **papier maché**
i) _____	i) e.g. cigarette boxes	i) e.g. _____
ii) e.g. quilted _____	ii) e.g. _____	ii) e.g. trays _____
iii) _____	iii) made of _____	iii) e.g. _____
	iv) inlaid _____	iv) painted with ____

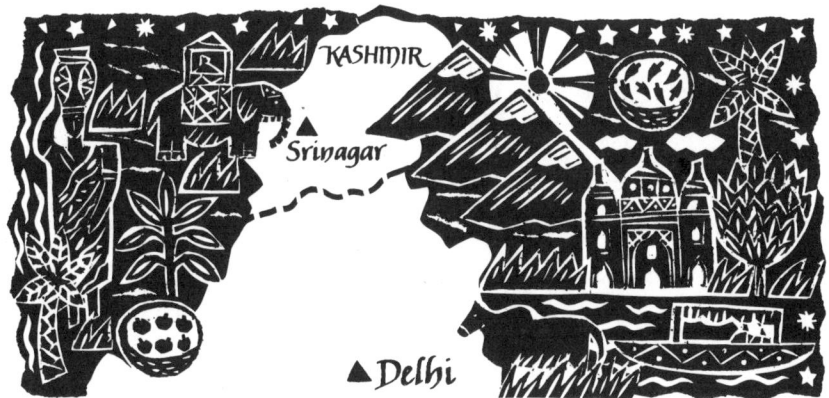

Follow-up

1 Describing a visit

Work in groups. Tell the group about a visit you have made to another country or to another part of your own country.
a) Where and when did you go?
b) Did you visit any places of special interest?
c) What kind of food did you have there?
d) Did you buy anything there?
e) Was there anything else you would have liked to buy?
f) Would you recommend other people to go there?

2 Planning a visit

Work in pairs.
a) Describe two places in your country that you think are worth visiting. Say where they are and how to get there.
b) Say what local or traditional things you think a visitor might like to buy there. Give their approximate price.
c) Ask your partner to choose one of the places to visit and one item to buy there. Ask your partner to give reasons for his or her choice.

Study point

1 Informal conversation

These are some common features of informal conversation.
a) people speaking at the same time
b) interruption
c) hesitation
d) repetition
e) rephrasing (saying the same thing in a different way)
f) incomplete sentences

Listen to this part of the conversation again and mark on the tapescript below the points where these features occur.

Liz: What about – didn't you say something about – before – about some gardens?
Marsha: Oh, the gardens. Yes.
Julia: Yes.
Marsha: There are dozens of Mogul gardens. We –
Liz: What are the Moguls?
Julia: Shalimar. Oh, Mogul.
Marsha: Mogul. That was from the Mogul period. That was – what – eighteenth century?
Julia: Yes.
Marsha: The Mogul emperors built these gardens and they have a –
Julia: Very formal.
Marsha: Yes. There's a pattern to all of them. With – there's a – they're on several levels – terraces. They're terraced.
Julia: Yes.

2 Advice and recommendation

Match **A** with **B** to complete the questions.

A	B
a) Would you recommend	absolutely unmissable?
b) Whereabouts would you suggest	me to spend my time?
c) When do you think	the northern part?
d) How would you advise	a visit?
e) What things are	I look for?
f) Is the museum worth	I go?
g) What sort of bargains should	buying?
h) Are the wood carvings worth	is the best time to go?

Think about the advice and recommendations that Julia and Marsha gave.
Now write long answers to the questions, like this:
a) I would recommend the northern part.

Writing A guide

Write a short guide advising visitors where to go, what to see and what to buy in your town or in another place you know well.

Before Breakfast

Before Breakfast is a short play. The two main characters are Tom, aged twenty-one and Joanna, aged nineteen. The action takes place in the dining car of a train.

'Coffee for both?'

Pre-listening

1 Describing your experiences

a) Do you usually talk to strangers on planes or trains?
b) Have you ever met anyone interesting on a plane or train journey?
c) Have you ever made new friends as a result of meeting someone in this way?
d) Can you remember a strange or frightening encounter with someone while travelling?

Extensive listening

2 Understanding gist

Are these statements true or false?
a) Tom and Joanna met seven years ago.
b) Joanna loved Tom then.
c) Tom remembers Joanna.
d) Joanna remembers Tom.
e) Joanna likes Tom now.
f) Tom likes Joanna.

Intensive listening

1 Listening for specific information

Tom says at the end that he and Joanna might get to like one another. What are the three, rather trivial, things we already know they both like?

a) They both _____
b) They both _____
c) They both _____

2 Focussing on tenses

Seven different tenses are used in this part of the dialogue. Put the verb in brackets into the correct tense.

Joanna: But we (BE) in love.
Tom: I never (BE) in love.
Joanna: Then you (LIE) to me. You (DECLARE) your undying passion.
Tom: Look. This (GET) embarrassing. The next thing you (TELL) me is that we (BE) married.

3 Appreciating humour

Tom often makes jokes. Sometimes he teases Joanna, sometimes he pretends not to understand her, sometimes he plays on words and sometimes he says something unexpected.
When Joanna asks Tom these questions, what does he say next? Can you understand his humour in each case?

a) *Can I sit down then?*
b) *You don't recognise me, do you?*
c) *Don't you recognise me from before? From a long time ago?*
d) *(Don't go.) Why shouldn't I?*

VOCABULARY

cut out to stop or exclude
get a bad press to be reported in a negative way in the media in general
cholesterol a fat-like substance found in the blood (a high level of cholesterol in the blood is a cause of heart disease)
cream tea tea served with scones (a kind of cake), jam and a thick cream (a speciality of Devon and Cornwall in the south-west of England)
peck a quick kiss, without much feeling
snap This is what British people say when two people do or say something at exactly the same time. This originates from a card game called *Snap*.
pompous foolishly serious and self-important

Follow-up

1 Giving your reactions

How did you react to Tom and Joanna? Would you describe either of them in any of these ways? Give your reasons.

clever	romantic	interesting	irritating
naive	boring	warm	cold
amusing	rude	shy	likeable

2 Giving your opinions

Tom and Joanna first met when they were adolescents. Now they are adults. How much do you think people change during their teenage years? Talk about yourself or someone you know as an example.

Study point

1 Formal and informal style

You will need to look at the tapescript or listen to the tape again to do this exercise. Joanna accuses Tom of being 'pompous'. This is because he often uses a very formal style when it would be more natural to be informal.

These are some examples of informal style. Write down how Tom says the same things but in more formal language.

a) I don't know that you do know my name.
b) So you do know my name. My first name, anyway.
c) I think you must have mixed me up with someone else.
d) I can't remember you at all.

These are some examples of a formal style. At the end of the play, Tom is sincere about his liking for Joanna and he begins to speak to her more naturally. Write down how he says the same things but in more informal language.

e) I feel that if we began as if this was our first meeting, then results might be different.
f) I think we might come to like each other quite considerably.

2 Idioms and colloquial language

Choose the correct meaning to match these idioms.

a) *You only live once.*
   i) You might as well enjoy it.
   ii) You should be careful.
b) *Doesn't the name ring a bell?*
   i) Don't you like my name?
   ii) Don't you remember my name?
c) *We started off on the wrong foot.*
   i) We started off at the wrong time.
   ii) We started off badly.

Writing   **Dialogue**

Choose one of the following situations and write a short dialogue.

a) Joanna and Tom meet for the first time. He is fourteen and she is twelve.

b) You start talking to a stranger on a train. After a while, you discover that you were at school together.

c) Someone comes to sit next to you on a train. The person knows your name and all about you, but you cannot remember him/her at all.

'I had pigtails.'

Looking Back

Peter, Barbara and John talk about their childhood.

Pre-listening

1 Describing your experience

Talk about your childhood in pairs or groups.
a) Do you come from a large or small family?
b) Are there any special family occasions which stand out in your memory of childhood?
c) Can you remember making any visits to the seaside or countryside?
d) Did you have any particular fears or anxieties as a child?
e) Did you have any pets?

Extensive listening

1 Listening for the main points

Which of the following topics is mentioned?

birthdays		a river		a grandfather	
a funeral		jobs		a grandmother	
a wedding		schooldays		an argument	
the countryside		shopping		a pet	

2 Understanding reference

Look at the words in italics. Which person, place, occasion or event is being referred to in each case?
a) **Peter:** When the tide was out, you could go down onto the sand *there*.
b) **Barbara:** *That's* got to be one of the highlights of my life.
c) **John:** *It* was mostly physical violence really.
d) **John:** *The poor old dear* almost had a premature heart attack.
e) **Peter:** And my poor father. He felt terrible about *it*.

Intensive listening

1 Listening for specific information

a) Peter's family lived in a one-bedroomed flat. How many people slept in the same bedroom?

3	4	5	6	

b) What was Barbara's bridesmaid's dress like?

plain pink		pink with flowers	
pink and red		pink with red stripes	

2 Guessing vocabulary from context

Listen to what John said about his childhood and then guess the meanings of the words below.
I was a very solitary sort of child. I suppose being an only child living in a very remote village contributed to this. I enjoyed my own company, I suppose.
a) '*an only child*' means
  i) a child with one brother or sister
  ii) a child with no brothers or sisters
b) '*remote*' means
  i) far from other towns or villages
  ii) near other towns or villages
I managed to acquire an old tatty pair of binoculars.
c) '*tatty*' means
  i) of poor appearance
  ii) of smart appearance

3 Checking comprehension

Are these statements true or false?
a) Peter was afraid of the dark.
b) He was also frightened of spiders.
c) Barbara had nightmares.
d) She was afraid she would die in her sleep.
e) Bullying was unusual at John's school.
f) Young boys were taken behind the bicycle sheds and hit.

4 Understanding implications

Who do you think might have said the following?

John	John's mother	John's grandmother
Peter	Peter's father	

a) Sorry. I didn't mean to give you a shock.
b) I'm so sorry. I didn't know it was there.
c) Oh. You frightened me.
d) Oh. You've killed it.
e) You mustn't do that again. You could have broken your leg.

Follow-up

1 Discussion

Work in groups. What do you think are the advantages and disadvantages for a child growing up in the following situations?
a) with brothers and sisters
b) as an only child
c) in a big city
d) in the countryside
Tell the class what your group thinks.

2 Making a survey

a) Complete the questionnaire below.

SURVEY: CHILDHOOD 1				
Do you remember having any of these experiences?				
	often	sometimes	occasionally	never
fear of the dark				
nightmares				
feeling lonely				
enjoying parties				
visiting relations				
enjoying holidays				

b) Find out how everyone in the class answered the questions. Summarise the most striking results of the survey like this:
More than half the class were sometimes afraid of the dark.
Only about five percent of the class often had nightmares.

c) In groups, make a similar questionnaire to find out what good and bad experiences people had during their schooldays. Ask another group to complete your questionnaire. Summarise your results as before.

Study point

1 Habitual past

Read these examples.

Habitual past actions/states:
My mum used to make lovely cakes.
They would go as far as stealing their pocket money.
My grandmother spent three months of the year with us.

Completed past actions/states:
When I was bridesmaid, I had this gorgeous dress on.
I had my father's umbrella and I leapt off the window sill and landed in front of my grandmother.
Note: 'Would' is more formal than 'used to'. It is more often used to describe actions and events than states.

'The budgie was hopping around . . .'

a) Read these extracts. Decide if habitual past behaviour or completed actions are being described. Now change the verbs in brackets into the 'used to' form where possible. Where this is not possible, use the Past Simple.

We (¹LIVE) in a one-bedroomed flat in London. In the summer, my mother (²TAKE) us down to the Thames.

Mostly we (³HAVE) budgies. Well, the saddest thing that (⁴HAPPEN) to one of our budgies was the time when it was playing on the floor with its toys. We often (⁵LET) it out of its cage and put its little toys on the floor. The budgie was hopping around on the floor and my father (⁶PUT) his feet down to go somewhere and (⁷TREAD) on the budgie. We (⁸BE) totally distraught.

b) With which verbs is it possible to use 'would'?

2 Non-standard forms

Both Barbara and Peter have London accents but Barbara also uses some common non-standard forms. These are also common in other regional dialects in Britain.

a) Look at these examples.
   This great big limousine come for me and me brother.
   We was sitting in the back and I was waving like the Queen.
   Now rewrite Barbara's sentences in standard English.

b) These sentences are in standard English but what did Barbara actually say?
   We were always round someone's house.
   It was all good fun when we were kids.
   I was frightened to close my eyes in case I'd die.

   Look at the tapescript or listen to the tape again to check your answers.

Writing   Description and narrative

a) Make sentences beginning as follows:

One of the	happiest memories highlights saddest occasions most ghastly moments	of my childhood was . . .

b) Now write two or three paragraphs about your own childhood.

The Long Essay

Selvi has written a draft plan for her long essay. She is discussing it with her tutor.

Pre-listening

1 Using information which is given

Read Selvi's plan. You can answer these questions about her already.
a) What kind of course is she doing?
b) Does she already have a University degree?
c) Is she from Britain?
d) What age group is she interested in?

2 Guessing further information

You might be able to guess the answers to these questions.
a) What is her job?
b) Where does she come from?

Postgraduate Diploma in English Studies	
LONG ESSAY/PROJECT	
TITLE	Materials to motivate students to communicate in English.
DESCRIPTION	For 7-11 year olds with parents from India, Pakistan, Japan and Hongkong; speaking mother tongue at home and the 2nd language (English) in the classroom. Type of materials – to include short stories and poems for practising phonetics. Local setting – a multi-cultural Junior school in North London – I have visited the school several times. (Q. Could my materials be used in my country too? There are some similarities.)

Extensive listening

1 Confirming your guesses

Check your answers to exercise 2 in the *Pre-listening*.

2 Listening for gist

Choose the correct way to complete these sentences.
a) During the tutorial, the title of Selvi's project is:
  i)   not changed
  ii) changed very little
  iii) changed considerably

b) Her new plan will include:
  i)   everything she had in her first draft
  ii) some of the points in her original plan
  iii) a completely new set of topics

c) At the end of the tutorial:
  i)   only Selvi is pleased
  ii) both Selvi and the tutor are pleased
  iii) only the tutor is pleased

Intensive listening

1 Listening for specific information

Which sentence is true?
a) Selvi wants to use poems which are already published.
b) She is going to write some poems herself.
c) She wants the children to write poems.

2 Note-taking

Use the plan below to do the following.
a) Complete the new title of Selvi's project.
b) Complete the section headings and sub-headings as indicated.

VOCABULARY

draft first, rough plan
mother tongue a person's native language
medium way of giving information
form class
background a person's family, experience or education
context the general conditions in which an event takes place
universal for all people or every purpose
criteria the principles on which a judgement is made
motivation a need or purpose for doing something
curricular relating to a course of study

TITLE .....Using a topic-based approach to the.........
.....teaching of...

DESCRIPTION

PART 1 .....CONTEXT.........................
  a) ....
  b) .....Malaysia...............................

PART 2 ....
  a) ....   ● ...poems.........
  b) ....   ● ....
  c) ...communicative.........................   ● ....
  d) ....
  e) ....

PART 3 ....

PART 4 ....

27

Follow-up

1 Role and function

Selvi is free to write the essay in the way she wants. The tutor's role is to help and advise.

Discuss these questions in pairs or groups.

a) You have heard only five minutes of a half-hour tutorial to discuss Selvi's long essay.
   What points do you think were discussed in the other twenty-five minutes? Make a list.

b) You heard the tutor talking more than the student. For which of the points you have listed, do you think Selvi talked more than the tutor?

2 Discussing plans

a) Work in pairs. Each of you choose a different essay topic from the list below.

| food | family life | road accidents | smoking |

b) Think of a more specific title.

c) Tell your partner how you will organise your essay. Explain what you will say in each part of the essay:
   - introduction
   - main sections
   - sub-sections
   - conclusion

d) Suggest ways to improve your partner's plan.

Study point

1 Making suggestions

Selvi's tutor avoids being too critical. Instead, she suggests what should be done in an encouraging way, often by using 'we' instead of 'you'. Rewrite the sentences below as indicated. Look at the tapescript or listen to the tape again to check your answers.

a) What you need is a much more specific plan.
Tutor: I think _____ we _____ slightly _____

b) You have to make a plan.
Tutor: Shall we see _____ we _____?

c) List the things you've mentioned.
Tutor: Let's _____ we _____

d) You must go through them.
Tutor: Can we _____?

e) Does that make sense – if I put it like that?
Tutor: _____ to you _____ we _____?

2 Prefixes

Complete these sentences using words formed with the following prefixes.

| re | bi | cross | mis | sub | multi |

All of the words except one have been used in this Unit.

a) Selvi wants to design teaching materials for use in _____ schools.

b) Most of these children are _____ . Some speak three or four languages.

c) The materials will be_____ so they can be used by teachers of different subjects.

d) The tutor _____ Selvi when she talked about using poems.
e) Each section of the essay will have several _____.
f) The tutor has not changed the content of the essay but she has _____ some of the points.

Look at the *Answer key* to check which words are spelt with a hyphen.

3 Foreign plurals

There are several words in this Unit which have foreign plurals. Look at the box below and fill in the missing words.

Nouns from	Singular	Plural
Greek	_____	criteria
	phenomenon	_____
	_____	hypotheses
	crisis	_____
Latin	medium	_____
	_____	curricula
	bacterium	_____

Writing An essay plan

a) Write a title and an essay plan on a topic which specially interests you.
b) When you are satisfied with your plan, write the first sentence for each section of your plan.

A Sense of Humour

Sandy is amusing his friends after lunch with some stories from Ireland and Scotland. Sandy is himself a Scot.

Pre-listening

1 Giving your opinion

a) How far is humour universal?
Can you give any examples of humour which you think everyone would find funny?

b) Do you think each country and nationality has a different sense of humour?
Are there things that make people laugh in your country which you think other nationalities might not understand even if they knew the language well?

c) Do you know anyone who makes people laugh a lot?
Which actors or comedians do you find funny?

Extensive listening

1 Explaining a joke

Which of the following statements best explains why the story about the swineherd is funny?

a) Sandy's friend thought it would be quicker to take the pigs by lorry but the swineherd thought it wouldn't make any difference to the journey.

b) Sandy's friend suggested that the swineherd use a lorry to take the pigs so that he could continue his journey by car.

c) Sandy's friend was thinking about the journey from the swineherd's point of view but the swineherd was thinking of the pigs' point of view.

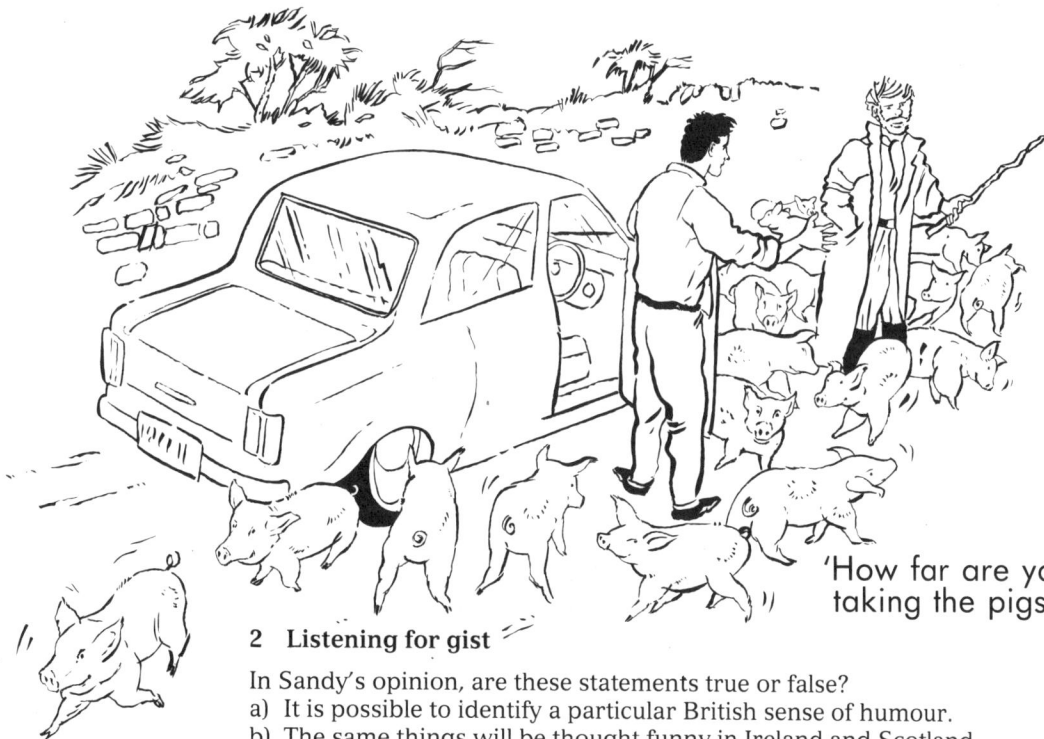

'How far are you taking the pigs?'

2 Listening for gist

In Sandy's opinion, are these statements true or false?
a) It is possible to identify a particular British sense of humour.
b) The same things will be thought funny in Ireland and Scotland.
c) Scottish humour often depends on the use of words.
d) A knowledge of linguistic and cultural background is not necessary to understand humour.
e) The stories he told about Ireland are good examples of the Irish character and sense of humour.

Intensive listening

1 Listening for specific expressions

Write down the expressions that are used at these points in the stories.
a) The swineherd suggests that time is not important to pigs.
b) The taxi driver explains that the funeral business is good in the winter because many people die then.

2 Focussing on vocabulary

Complete the gaps.

I think there are ^{1}_____ senses of humour and they're all very different. I think that one of the ^{2}_____ with humour in Great Britain – is that things that ^{3}_____ people as funny in Scotland, for example, wouldn't ^{4}_____ the Irish as particularly funny because they're nearly all ^{5}_____ on words using sometimes dialect ^{6}_____.

3 Giving examples of usage

How might a Scots person say these sentences?
a) I am not going.
b) He's not coming today.
c) Won't you come back again?
   What did the lady in the flower shop say? Complete her sentence.
d) Do you _____ _____ _____ _____ Nannette?

4 Understanding a joke

What is the joke one of Sandy's friends makes at the end?

31

Follow-up

1 Giving your reactions

a) Which of the three stories that Sandy told did you find most amusing: the one about the swineherd, the taxi driver or the lady in the flower shop?

b) Which of these reasons do you think helped you enjoy the story?

- It is similar to a joke or story you have heard before.
- The way Sandy tells it is very funny.
- You understood all the words and expressions.
- Sandy explains things you did not know before.
- You can picture the people in the story.
  Or was there another reason why you enjoyed the story?

2 Telling funny stories

Work in groups.

a) Take it in turns to tell a funny story or a joke you know.

b) Decide whose story or joke most people thought was the funniest. Why do you think this was?

c) Tell your group's best joke or story to the class. Which group has the funniest joke or story?

Study point

1 Relative clauses

a) Use the correct relative pronoun 'who' or 'which/that' to join each pair or group of sentences to make one sentence.

  i) I know a true story. It epitomises the Irish sense of humour.

  ii) It was a friend of mine. He was working in the south of Ireland.

  iii) There are regional senses of humour. They are all very different.

  iv) It is a musical comedy. It was written in the twenties.

  v) A person was singing with an opera company. The company was on tour in Edinburgh.

  vi) He went in a flower shop to buy some flowers for a friend. The friend was going on to do the performance that night.

b) Now rewrite your sentences without using the relative pronoun. Think about the changes you will have to make.

2 Direct and indirect speech

When Sandy tells these stories, he frequently uses direct speech to make the people in the stories come alive and to make the stories more dramatic and amusing.

This description of the opera singer's conversation with the lady in the flower shop uses indirect speech.

The lady in the flower shop asked the singer if he was in show business and he told her that he was. She said she had thought so. You could always tell. Sandy's friend expressed polite surprise at this. The lady went on to explain that she used to be in show business herself. The singer showed polite interest. Then the lady told him that she had been in 'No No Nannette'. When the singer looked completely blank at this because he had never heard of it, she asked with surprise if he did not know 'No No Nannette'.

Rewrite their conversation in direct speech. Begin like this:
Lady: Excuse me. _____?
Singer: Yes, _____.

Writing   Review

Write a short review for a newspaper or magazine of a film, play, show or book that you found particularly funny. Quote some of the dialogue or lines if you can.

or

Write an amusing story you know.

A Card Trick

Magicians are not
supposed to give away
their secrets but Bert
Coules agreed to explain
how to do one simple
card trick.
It will be useful if you
have a pack of cards for
this Unit.

Pre-listening

1 Learning topic-related vocabulary

If you want to play cards or to do a card trick, you will need to know the
names of the four suits and the names of the face cards.

ace   king   queen   jack or knave   hearts   diamonds   clubs   spades

What is the name of the card in each of the pictures below?

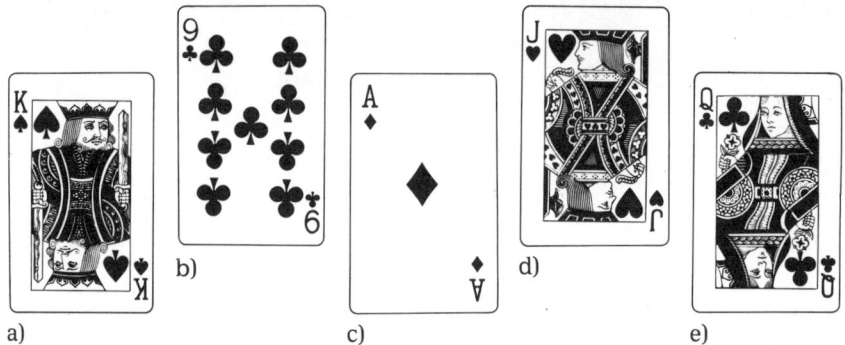

a)

b)

c)

d)

e)

How do you tell someone to do these actions?

f)

Please _____ the cards.

g)

Please _____ the cards.

Extensive listening

1 Understanding key points

All of these statements are true but which two statements are the key to understanding how the trick is done?
a) The other person has to shuffle the cards.
b) The magician has to look at the bottom card of the pack.
c) The other person mustn't see the magician looking at the bottom card.
d) The other person cuts the pack in half.
e) The magician pretends to read the other person's mind.
f) When the magician finds the card, he or she asks the other person to turn it over.

Intensive listening

1 Following instructions

These are some of the things the magician will say at different points during the trick.

Put the sentences in the correct order.
a) Now please look at the top card of the ones I'm holding.
b) This is your card! Am I right?
c) Would you shuffle the cards, please?
d) Remember this card and put it on top of the cards you are holding.
e) Now you must concentrate and think very hard of your card.
f) Now I'm going to put my half of the pack on top of yours and bury your card in the middle of the pack.
g) Please cut the cards.

2 Checking comprehension

Give short answers to these questions.
a) Should the magician secretly look at the bottom card of the pack before or after the other person has cut the cards?
b) Is squaring up the cards on the table a good way to look at the bottom card or is it too obvious?
c) Does the magician pretend to read the other person's mind near the beginning of the trick or at the end?
d) Is the other person's card above or below the card the magician has seen?

Follow-up   1   Tricks and puzzles

Work in pairs.

a) Arrange ten coins to form a triangle, like this:

This triangle is pointing upwards. Can you make the triangle point downwards by moving only three coins? If you can, tell your partner how to do it. If not, look at page 86 to find out.

b) Ask your partner to follow these instructions.

- Open this book at any page.
- Choose any line on the page from 1 to 9.
- Choose any word on the line from 1 to 9.
- Double the number of the page.
- Multiply the answer by 5 and add 20.
- Add the number of the line plus 5.
- Multiply by 10.
- Add the number of the word in the line.
- Subtract 250 from the total.
- What is your total figure now?

From this figure, you can find the word your partner chose.
Look at page 86 to find out how you can do this. Now explain it to your partner.

c) Do you know any other tricks or puzzles? If you know a trick, try it on the other students. Can they guess how it's done? Will you tell them the secret?

Study point

1 Giving instructions

These are some of the words and phrases Bert used to give instructions.

You've *got to* . . .
You *have to* . . .
If you . . ., you *can't* . . .
This is the moment when . . .
A good way to do it is to . . .

Don't . . .
Please . . .
You *need* . . .
You *must* . . .

Now use the words and phrases in italics to complete his sentences. Use each word or phrase only once.

a) You _____ two things – a pack of cards and a person to show the trick to.

b) _____ cut the cards. You _____ look at the bottom card and remember what it is.

c) _____ show it to me. I mustn't see it.

d) You _____ remember. _____ you forget, you _____ do the trick.

e) _____ to take the cards and pretend to be squaring them up.

f) _____ when I ask you to think very hard of the card.

g) You've _____ take my mind away from what you're doing.

2 Understanding reference

What is the pronoun '*it*' or '*that*' referring to in each of these cases? Write your answers like this:
(**a**) '*it*' refers to . . .

Right. Now I've found the card that I saw, but – so – your card must be next to (**a**) *it,* but will (**b**) *it* be above my card or below?
You have to look at the bottom card of the pack and remember what (**c**) *it* is. You have to do that secretly so that (**d**) *it* is not obvious. Okay. I'll have to practise (**e**) *that,* but I've seen (**f**) *it* now.

Writing

Instructions

Written instructions must be very clear and easy to follow. It is helpful to do the following:

- keep sentences short
- list and number instructions
- use headings when there are separate sections
- use the imperative form as often as possible.

a) Write a short set of instructions for one of the following:

| serving in tennis | planting a tree | making tea |
| cooking rice | wiring a plug | using a shampoo |

b) Now think of something that you know how to do that another student does not. Write instructions and give them to the other student. Ask him or her if they are clear. Explain any parts that are not clear. Rewrite the instructions if necessary.

The Macbeth Ordeal

The Macbeth Ordeal is based on a true story that happened a few years ago. It all started when Gerry, an actor, was offered the part of Macbeth.

'Macbeth should have a beard.'

Pre-listening

1 Thinking about what you know

Can you answer these questions?
a) Who wrote the play *Macbeth*?
b) Where does the play take place?
c) In the play, who is Macbeth?
If you cannot answer these questions now, look at them again when you have listened to the tape.

2 Drawing on your own experience

a) Are you superstitious? Are many people in your country superstitious?
b) Are certain numbers or dates considered to be lucky or unlucky in your country?
c) What other things are thought to bring good or bad luck?

Extensive listening

1 Listening for gist

Choose the correct way to complete the sentence.
After agreeing to play the part of Macbeth,
a) Gerry decided to break up with his girlfriend.
b) Gerry had a lot of bad luck.
c) Gerry predicted he would have a lot of problems.

2 Following a story

Number these pictures in the order they show what happened in the story.

a)

b)

c)

d)

e)

f)

3 Making inferences

When did Gerry feel like this?

a) eager   b) stubborn   c) apologetic   d) ill
e) cold   f) relieved   g) shocked   h) resigned

Intensive listening

1 Listening for specific details

Gerry wants us to think that he is not superstitious. However, there are two things he does which suggest that he is superstitious. What are they?

VOCABULARY

ordeal a difficult experience
quote lines to say the words of a play
title role the main part in a play
premonition a feeling that something is going to happen, usually something unpleasant
hilarious very funny
break up to end a relationship
predictable possible to be known in advance
attic the part of a house just below the roof
asthma an illness which makes breathing very difficult
gasp to breathe with difficulty
chilly cold
deserted without people

2 Understanding idioms

Listen to the tape again and notice when these idioms are used. Now choose the correct meaning.

a) *'on your own head be it'* means
   i)   You must take responsibility for this action.
   ii) You must change your mind.
   iii) You are to blame.

b) *'one of those days'* means
   i)   a day when the weather is bad
   ii) a day when the trains are late
   iii) a day when everything goes wrong

c) *'I'm not crazy about them'* means
   i)   I think they are mad.
   ii) I don't like them very much.
   iii) I hate them.

Follow-up

1 Cultural background

a) When Gerry saw the cats, he crossed his fingers. Why did he do this? What do people do for the same reason in your country?
b) Gerry says his beard had 'a considerable amount of red in it' and it was 'highly appropriate for a Scottish king'. Why does he say this?
c) He says, 'There was bound to be a hotel open somewhere – even in Inverness'. Why does he say, 'even in Inverness'?

2 Story-telling

You have only heard half of Gerry's story. Work in groups to continue the story.
a) How was the incident in the hotel resolved? Did Gerry have to go to the police station? Did they find the real thief?
   Tell the class how your group finished the story.
b) Do you have an 'unlucky story' about yourself that you can tell?

Study point

1 Connectives

Use the words in the box to complete Gerry's sentences. Use each word once.

| but   so   nevertheless   although   and   as   despite   however |

a) It is considered to be extremely unlucky. _____ when I was offered the title role, I jumped at the chance of playing it _____ the warnings of my superstitious girlfriend.
b) We had so little in common that quarrelling was a way of passing the time. My beard, _____, was a great success.
c) The train left Kings Cross on time _____ after that there was an endless series of delays.
d) There were no buses at that time of night _____ I had to take a taxi.
e) I apologised for arriving so late _____ Alison led me upstairs to my room.
f) I have a problem with cats. It's not that I don't like them. _____ I'm not crazy about them.
g) _____ I filled in the registration form, I told him my story.

2 Past perfect

Put the verbs in brackets in the correct tense: Past Simple or Past Perfect. You will also have to decide whether to use the Past Perfect Continuous or not. All the sentences are taken from Gerry's story.

a) Three weeks later, I no longer (HAVE) a girlfriend . . . We (SPEND) a lot of our time quarrelling.
b) I finally (ARRIVE) in Inverness at one o'clock in the morning. I (TRAVEL) for nearly twelve hours.
c) I (WAKE) up gasping for breath. The cats probably (PLAY) in the bedclothes.
d) Suddenly there was a scream. I (TURN) round and (SEE) a woman who I (ASSUME) to be the manager's wife.

'Hello, Bushytail.'

Writing **Narrative**

a) Write two more paragraphs to continue Gerry's story of things that went wrong. Try not to use direct speech.

b) Write a story of your own called 'One of those Days'.

Office Life

The staff of this busy office spend much of their time on the telephone. Joanna, the office manager talks about their work.

Pre-listening

1 Giving your opinions

a) Do you think working in an office is a boring job? Give your reasons.
b) What qualities do you think you need to be good at working on the phone?
c) A personal secretary works for one particular boss. What special responsibilities do you think he or she has?

2 Predicting language

What would you say on the telephone in these situations.
a) You want to speak to John Smith.
b) You want to say who you are.
c) You ask someone to wait.
d) The person you want is not there, so you want to leave a message.
e) The message is that you want him to ring you back.

Extensive listening

1 Listening for the main points

a) Which of these kinds of phone calls did you hear?
   i) an inter-departmental call
   ii) an outside call
   iii) a personal call
b) Which of the following did you hear someone doing?
   i) leaving a message
   ii) making an appointment
   iii) asking for information
   iv) making a complaint
   v) dealing with a problem

2 Making inferences

Do you think Joanna, the office manager, would agree or disagree with these statements?
a) You may need more patience if you're talking to a member of the public than if the call is inter-departmental.
b) A private secretary should never pretend that the boss is not there.
c) The atmosphere in the office is not serious enough.
d) It is up to you and your colleagues whether working in an office is boring or not.

Intensive listening

1 Listening for specific information

Complete these messages.

a)

To: Geoff Corbett

From: _____

Please phone her on extension _____
She wants to book some _____
in and she has a _____

b)

To:

From: Cathy

The account number you
wanted is 4 _____ _____

2 Focussing on vocabulary

Complete the gaps.

Working in an office, part of the ¹_____ is dealing with ²_____ and today we did have a particular problem. It was something to do with a ³_____ worker. I'm not sure exactly what the problem was but no doubt we'll ⁴_____ it out.

3 Checking comprehension

Kay phoned Vera about a problem with some employees' payments. Choose the correct way to complete these sentences.

a) The salary cheque was   i) correct.
                               ii) incorrect.

b) The invoice is   i) correct.
                      ii) incorrect.

c) i) Both Vera and Kay   change/s the invoice.
    ii) Only Kay

Follow-up

1 Giving your reactions

Work in groups.
a) What do you think the advantages and disadvantages might be of working in this particular office? Make two lists.
b) Compare your reactions with other groups'.

2 Passing on messages

a) Three or four students should each think of a message to give to another student sitting in another part of the classroom.
b) These students should whisper their message to the person sitting next to them who passes it on to the next student and so on.
c) When each message has reached the person it was intended for, those students should repeat the message for everyone to hear. The person who sent it can check that it is correct.

Study point

1 Speaking on the telephone

a) Complete this telephone conversation.

Caller: _____ me _____ 3044, please?
Secretary: Hullo. Accounts.
Caller: _____ John Mellor, please?
Secretary: _____ moment.
Hullo. I'm _____ not in his office at the moment.
Caller: _____ when he's likely to be back?
Secretary: In about an hour. _____ a message?
Caller: Just _____ Mary Slade phoned and _____ ring me back.
Secretary: Does he have your number?
Caller: No. It's _____
Secretary: 948.
Caller: _____
Secretary: 3266. All right. I'll see that he gets the message.
Caller: Thank you. Goodbye.

b) Which sentence in each pair is more informal than the other?
i) Is he in the office today?
Is he around today?
ii) Just a moment.
Just one moment.
iii) Can you hold on for a second?
Can you hang on a second?
iv) Sorry. I've no idea where he is.
I'm afraid I don't know where he is at the moment.
v) It's Mary Slade here.
My name is Mary Slade.
Which of these sentences do you think you would use when speaking to a friend or colleague, your boss or someone you have never met before?

2 Business vocabulary

Use the words in the box to complete the sentences below. You may have to change the form of the word.

---

order overtime invoice account charge net gross quote

---

a) We're going to buy the products from Japan because their _____ is much lower. I'm sure they'll get _____ from other countries too.
b) This statement is not correct because the fees were _____ to the wrong _____ .
c) We've received the goods but you haven't sent us an _____ .
d) His _____ salary seems high but after he's paid tax and insurance it's difficult to support a family on his _____ earnings.
e) In many industries, the basic rates of pay are so low that _____ is routine for many workers.

Writing Messages

a) Write down a telephone message for Joanna, the office manager. Make sure your message includes the following information:
 • who the message is from
 • what information is given
 • what action is required
 • the date and time the message was received

b) Write another telephone message for someone in your class.

The Exhibition

The Ideal Home Exhibition is held at Earls Court, London every year. It has displays and demonstrations of all kinds of household equipment.

Pre-listening

1 Expressing your own preferences

a) If you were at this exhibition, which kind of furniture would you like to look at?

b) Would you prefer to look at the products on your own or to hear a salesman describe or demonstrate them? Why?

c) Make a list of six pieces of equipment, large or small, that you have in your kitchen. Which is the most useful item? What other kitchen equipment would you like to have?

2 Predicting content

a) What kind of information do you think is given to visitors at the exhibition on the public announcement system?

b) Write two public announcements which you might hear at the exhibition.

Extensive listening

1 Recognising different speakers

a) How many public announcements are made? Are any of them the ones you predicted?

b) How many salesmen do you hear?

2 Listening for gist

Which salesman emphasises which of these selling points? Tick the appropriate box.

Selling points	Salesman A (tin opener)	Salesman B (polish)	Salesman C (water beds)
economical			
safe			
healthy			
multi-purpose			
popular			

Intensive listening

1 Focussing on vocabulary

The organiser does not remember any exact figures about the exhibition. Complete the gaps with the words and phrases she uses to show that her figures are approximate.

a) We have _____ half a million square feet of floor space.

b) We have _____ four hundred exhibitors each year.

c) And the number of people visiting – we expect _____ a million.

d) It'll be, I suppose, this year _____ eight hundred thousand.

2 Understanding implications

Read these sentences about the man who bought the 'miracle knife'.
Are the statements true or false?

a) The man often buys things from salesmen.

b) If the salesman had not been so persuasive, he might not have bought the knife.

c) He would have bought the knife even if it had been expensive.

d) He is angry with himself for having bought the knife.

e) He is amused because the demonstration impressed him so much.

f) The knife will be useful when he redecorates his kitchen.

3 Listening for specific information

Give advice to the Brown family. Answer 'Yes' or 'No'.

a) Should Mr and Mrs Brown go to the Child Playcare Centre to find their son Mathew?

b) Could they have left Mathew at the Child Playcare Centre while they looked round the exhibition?

c) Can Mr Brown get advice about a bank loan at the exhibition?

d) Mrs Brown has £1.20 in her purse. Has she got enough to buy a catalogue?

VOCABULARY

catalogue a list of names or products, usually with information about them
exhibitor a company or person who exhibits
magnet a piece of iron that draws other objects to it
rim the outside edge, especially of a round object
jugular a large blood vessel; there is one on each side of the neck
formica strong plastic often used for table tops
hide animal skins
convince to persuade
take in to deceive or cheat
cautious careful
Stanley knife a heavy knife with a sharp blade which can be moved in and out of the handle
chiropractor a person who treats diseases by feeling and pressing the bones, especially in the back and neck

Follow-up

1 Evaluating what you hear

a) How good do you think these salesman were?
Use the key below to give your rating for each salesman.

Key	
√ √	Yes, very much.
√	Yes, a bit.
×	No, not much.
× ×	No, not at all.

	Salesman A (tin opener)	Salesman B (polish)	Salesman C (water beds)
Were you amused?			
Were you informed?			
Were you persuaded?			

Compare your rating with another student's.

b) Have you given any of the salesmen √ or √ √? Explain what the salesmen said that you thought was amusing, informative or persuasive.

2 Sharing your experiences

Work in groups and compare your answers.

a) Are you easily impressed or usually cautious about people selling things?

b) Have you ever been taken in by a salesman or an advertisement? How were you persuaded?

c) Have you ever bought something you regretted buying later?

Study point

1 Persuasion

These are some of the ways by which salesmen try to persuade people to buy things.

i) Being very dramatic.

ii) Claiming the product is unique.

iii) Quoting statistics.

iv) Emphasising truthfulness.

v) Quoting scientists or other experts.

vi) Repeating phrases, often in threes.

All the examples below are taken from the salesmen you have just heard. Which of the above techniques of selling are they using in each case?
a) In actual fact, the magnet stops the lid going in the tin.
b) Unlike any other tin opener, you can actually walk round the kitchen.
c) I could take that right across my jugular and never ever cut myself.
d) (What happens if you stick a pin in it?)
   Well, then it would leak. It would cry like a little baby. It would come out like a tear drop.
e) Chiropractors in Canada send people to our stores to buy water beds.
f) In Norway – there's four point two million people live there – and they bought seventy-seven thousand water beds. In Canada we have twenty-two percent of the population sleeping on water.

2 Vocabulary sets

a) These seven verbs are all associated with liquids in some way.

> pour leak drain squirt squeeze suck wring

Use the appropriate verb to complete the salesmen's sentences.
   i) You can go over to the sink and _____ off the tin at any time.
   ii) You _____ a drop of polish into a bowl or saucer.
   iii) You only need a damp cloth so don't just _____ it out,
        _____ it out.
   iv) Animal skins – they're like a sponge and they'll just _____ it up.
   v) If you stick a pin in it, it would _____ .
   vi) The water is not under pressure. It won't _____ out.

b) Now try to use each verb in another example of your own.
c) Do you know any other verbs associated with liquids?

Writing Advertisements

Write an advertisement for one of the following:

- inflatable arm-bands (for children learning to swim)
- a new kind of toothpaste dispenser
- a device for washing bottles
- a soap dish
- a window cleaning liquid

The News

This is not a recent news broadcast but you can hear very similar events reported today.

ULSTER

TAIWAN

Pre-listening

1 Predicting vocabulary

a) Look at the photographs above.
   What do you think has happened in each case?
b) For each photograph, make a list of the vocabulary you might expect to hear in a report describing such an event.

Extensive listening

1 Understanding organisation

Number the four sections of the news in the order you hear them.

UK news	traffic report
world news	foreign correspondent's report

2 Listening for the main points

a) Which of the topics below is in the news?

b) Which one is the main news item?

an earthquake	a hi-jack	
drugs	political violence	
a fight in a pub	a typhoon	
an international agreement	a plane crash	
a road acccident	a strike	

3 Understanding implications

How do you think these people were feeling after listening to the news? Choose the appropriate word from the box.

pleased	worried	disappointed	frustrated

a) **Mrs Beale**
Her husband is a member of the RUC in County Antrim and he has not come home from work yet. She expected him back two hours ago.
b) **Joseph Doyle**
He is a drugs squad officer in the New York police department.
c) **Mr Gilpin**
His British firm has been negotiating for oil prospecting rights in India.
d) **Mary Hanlon**
She is a sales representative planning to drive south from Preston in Lancashire to Birmingham.

Intensive listening

1 Guessing vocabulary from context

Choose the correct meaning of these words.

a) *'casualty'* means
 i) damage to property
 ii) a person who is hurt accidentally
 iii) a person who helps injured people

b) *'hampered'* means
 i) made easier
 ii) made impossible
 iii) made more difficult

c) *'guarantees'* means
 i) suggests
 ii) promises
 iii) insists

d) *'factions'* means
 i) armies
 ii) leaders
 iii) groups

VOCABULARY

correspondent a newspaper, TV or radio reporter who reports from a distant place
seize to take by force or by official order
Ulster Northern Ireland (Note: the United Kingdom of Great Britain and Northern Ireland)
RUC Royal Ulster Constabulary (the police force)
loyalist a person who wants Northern Ireland to remain part of the United Kingdom
republican a person who wants Northern Ireland to become part of the Republic of Ireland (Eire)
parade a procession or march
civilian a person not in the armed forces or police
stable not changing or moving
in custody held by police
witness a person who sees something happening
congestion an overcrowded or blocked condition

2 Checking comprehension

Choose the correct item to complete the sentences.
a) The part-time policeman in Northern Ireland
 i) was hit in a car.
 ii) was shot at from a car.
 iii) shot at a car.

b) In Stoke
 i) one man was hurt and one killed.
 ii) two men were seen with knives.
 iii) two men are being held by police.

c) Mr Williams
 i) knew he was growing a drug, but thought the plants looked nice.
 ii) didn't know that cannabis is a drug.
 iii) didn't realise he was growing cannabis.

d) Drivers were told
 i) the warning signals were not working.
 ii) to take extra care when they saw the warning signals.
 iii) to approach junction 32 with extra care.

Follow-up

1 Oral summary

a) In groups, make a list of events which have been in the news recently and discuss what you know about them.

b) Each student should choose one news item from the list and make notes of the most important facts, i.e. who/what/when/where.

c) Use your notes to give a brief oral summary of the news item.

d) Decide on the best order for your group's news.

e) Now listen to another group giving their reports.

Study point

1 The passive

a) The passive is often used in news broadcasts. What reasons can you suggest for this?

b) Make sentences in the passive using the tense indicated in brackets, like this:

Five hundred houses/wash away/by floods (Past)
Five hundred houses were washed away by floods.

All the sentences are taken from the news you heard in this Unit.

i)	Two passenger ferries/sink	(Past Perfect)
ii)	A part-time policeman/injure	(Present Perfect)
iii)	He/hit/by shots fired from a car	(Past)
iv)	Two motor bikes/set/on fire	(Past)
v)	Drivers/ask/to take extra care	(Present)

2 Style and vocabulary

News reports often use vocabulary which gives a strong or dramatic effect. Look at the differences between these sentences.

i) Typhoon Wayne came to the west coast yesterday.
ii) Typhoon Wayne reached the west coast.
iii) Typhoon Wayne hit the west coast.
iv) Typhoon Wayne struck the west coast.

Sentences i) and ii) are neutral while iii) and iv) are more dramatic. Sentence iv) was used in the news you heard in this Unit.

a) Put these verbs into pairs with similar meanings and make a list, like this:

erupt	tear	smash	break	disrupt	rip	cripple	break out

You may need to use a dictionary.

Neutral	Strong/dramatic
reach	strike

b) Now use the more dramatic verbs to complete these sentences. Make sure the verbs are in the correct form. All the sentences are taken from the news you heard in this Unit.

   i)   The typhoon _____ across central Taiwan yesterday.

  ii) Communications in many areas were _____.

 iii) Violence _____ in Ulster last night.

 iv) The windows of two pubs and three houses were _____.

Writing   News reports

a) Write a short report of another disaster you have heard about. It can be a natural disaster or one caused by human error. Your report should be in a neutral style.

b) Now write another report of the same disaster. This time use a more dramatic style.

Sing Jazz

(*From left to right*)
Shirin, Paul, Ken, Donna
and Catherine go to a
jazz singing class every
Saturday at their local
arts centre.

Pre-listening

1 Thinking about what you know and like

a) What is jazz? Do you know of any well-known jazz singers or
musicians?
b) What kind of music do you like – pop, jazz, folk or classical?
c) Can you play a musical instrument? Do you enjoy singing yourself?

Extensive listening

1 Listening for the main points

Which of these reasons for coming to the class do the singers mention?

to learn more about jazz	to make a lot of money	
to learn to sing louder	to earn a living as a singer	
to learn to play an instrument	to write new songs	
to become a teacher	to be as good as possible	
to express themselves through music	to sing with or for other people	

2 Understanding different speakers

Use 'All', 'Some', 'One' or 'None' to complete these sentences.
a) _____ of these singers want to learn more.
b) _____ of them are ambitious professionally.
c) _____ of them think they are perfect singers.
d) _____ of them sounds older than the others.
e) _____ of them seem to be having a good time.

Intensive listening

1 Checking comprehension

Choose the correct way to complete these sentences.
a) Shirin, the first speaker,
   i)   has just been given a job.
   ii) has decided to work hard at improving her singing.
   iii) thinks she needs more professional experience.

b) Donna and Catherine
   i)   want to know more about jazz singing.
   ii) can only sing jazz styles.
   iii) want to sing like each other.

c) All his life, Ken has
   i)   had many opportunities to sing.
   ii) performed in front of many people.
   iii) only had the chance to sing at home until now.

2 Focussing on vocabulary

Complete the missing words.
a) And, er, the _____ to take a song which has been written maybe I don't know how many years ago and sung many times and make it your _____ because you can bring something _____ to a song.
b) You've got a lot of freedom to do what you want and be _____ but within certain _____ .

3 Understanding a joke

Ken says his voice is '*not all that marvellous*'. The others disagree and say '*rubbish*'. What is the joke Ken makes then?

Follow-up

1 Asking questions

In this Unit, you did not hear the interviewer. Write down five questions which you think the singers were asked.

2 Discussion

a) Number these qualities in the order you think they are important for a jazz singer to be successful.

ambition	a good voice
confidence	an ability to read music
a sense of rhythm	a sense of humour
a love of music	a willingness to practise

b) Do you think the singers on the tape have any of these qualities? Give your reasons.

3 Giving opinions

Choose another kind of music, or a sport or another activity which you enjoy either as a participant or as an observer. Make a list of the qualities you think are needed for someone to become successful at this activity.

Study point

1 Word formation

Complete the chart below. You have heard all the missing words on the tape.

Noun	Adjective	Adverb
_____	flexible	flexibly
_____	vocal	_____
rhythm	rhythmical	_____
_____	_____	technically
_____	expressive	expressively
creativity	_____	creatively
_____	_____	emotionally

2 Fillers

In conversational English, 'fillers' such as those listed below are frequently used.

well   actual   actually   you know   I mean

Put in the most appropriate filler at each point indicated below.
a) yeah _____ the technical side is certainly a challenge and was a big challenge to me to learn the _____ technique but it was also very good to _____ put emotion into it
b) yeah _____ _____ I haven't got an incredibly good instrument in my voice and not all that marvellous a voice _____

Look at the tapescript on pages 78–79 to check what was said.

Writing

Short essays

Write a short essay of about two hundred words about something you enjoy doing very much. It might be something you do at work, something you are studying or perhaps a hobby.
Say:

- why you enjoy it
- what qualities a person needs to do it successfully
- what qualities and weaknesses you think you have
- what ambitions you have.

Remember to start a new paragraph when you move on to a new section of the essay.

On the Agenda

Students of the City Polytechnic film club are holding a committee meeting.
(*From left to right* Meg, Steve, Brian and Carol.)

Pre-listening

1 Giving your opinions

a) What responsibilities do the Chair, Secretary and Treasurer have?
b) Would you like to take on any of these responsibilities?
c) Do you think that meetings are boring sometimes? Why is this?

2 Using information which is given

Look at the letter to the committee members on page 59.
a) Is the meeting at the beginning or end of the academic year?
b) Is it a meeting for all the members of the club?
c) Where is the meeting being held?
d) What do you think the missing items on the agenda might be?

Extensive listening

1 Listening for sequence

These are the missing items on the agenda.

elections	minutes of meeting of May 20th	financial matters
date of next meeting	matters arising	next year's programme

Add these items to the agenda in the correct order.

2 Checking comprehension

Are these statements true or false?
a) Meg complained about her exam timetable.
b) Everyone voted for the film, *Knife in the Water*.
c) Steve voted for the film, *Butch Cassidy and the Sundance Kid*.
d) Carol does not know the club's rules as well as Brian.
e) The meeting could not reach a decision about the date of the next committee meeting.
f) Carol forgot to ask if there was any other business.

CITY POLYTECHNIC
Film Club

Dear Committee Member

There will be a meeting of the Committee on Tuesday June 30th at 7.15 pm in Room 2 in the Students' Union. This is mainly to discuss Item 4.

Please try to come.

Brian Hill

Brian Hill
Secretary

AGENDA

1 Apologies

2 _____

3 _____

4 _____

5 _____

6 _____

7 _____

8 AOB

Intensive listening

1 Focussing on vocabulary

Complete the gaps with the words Meg used.

Well, I'm afraid I've got a [1]_____ to make about this. I – as you know – I [2]_____ the meeting before last because I had flu. And I couldn't believe that the date of the last meeting was [3]_____ for May the twentieth. It's just – it's such a [4]_____ time to choose. We were all [5]_____. I couldn't get to it because I'd got an exam the next day and no [6]_____ I was going to [7]_____ that.

2 Understanding attitude and implication

a) Which film does each of these comments refer to, directly or indirectly: *Knife in the Water* or *Butch Cassidy and the Sundance Kid*?
b) What attitude towards the film does the speaker have in each case: positive or negative?

   i) *We must go for . . .*
   ii) *a very good example of a genre picture*
   iii) *a good laugh*
   iv) *You can get that from a video library.*
   v) *foreign, serious, heavy*
   vi) *nice, light, jokey*
   vii) *a well-made film*
   viii) *a good example of film technique*

3 Listening for specific information

Give one word answers to these questions.
a) In which week of October should the next committee meeting be?
b) What date is suggested?
c) What time does the Union meeting start?
d) What time will the film club committee meeting start?
e) Do they think members will be more or less likely to attend a committee meeting at that time?

Follow-up

1 Planning a meeting

Work in groups. Each group is a student club.
a) Decide what your club is for.
b) Nominate and elect a Chair, Secretary and Treasurer.
c) Decide on the rules of your club. For example, think about the membership, fees, aims and number of meetings per term/year.
d) Write an agenda for your next meeting.

2 Holding a meeting

Continue working in groups. Hold a meeting to discuss the agenda you have just written. You may wish to look at the *Study point*, exercise 1, before you begin your meeting. Make notes on the main points discussed and agreed during the meeting.

Study point

1 Agreement and disagreement

Complete these phrases and sentences with one word only for each gap.
a) I'd like to _____ the meeting _____ they agree on this.
_____ anybody got anything _____ to say?
b) I think that's fair _____.
It _____ very reasonable to me.
That's a good _____.
_____ly. I agree.
c) Does _____ have any opinions about this?
What does everybody else _____ _____ this?
d) I'm afraid I would _____ with you there.
You see, it's a _____ of timing.
The _____ is, you see, we have to plan ahead.
Right. _____ taken.
e) Everyone has had a _____.
I think we'd better _____ it to a vote.
Who's _____? Right. And who's_____?

2 Reporting a meeting

On the opposite page are the minutes of the Film Club's meeting of June 30th. What verb form do you think is often used in minutes? Why? Put the verbs below into the appropriate form to complete this report of the meeting.

> take   make   hold   propose   second   read
> receive   point   agree   decide   attend   remind

Writing   Minutes

Look back at the agenda and the notes you wrote in the *Follow-up* activities. Now write the minutes of the meeting you held. Compare your minutes with other students' in your 'club'.

CITY POLYTECHNIC
Film Club

MINUTES - JUNE 30

Apologies for absence [1] _____ from the Treasurer. The meeting [2] _____ by four committee members. The minutes of the previous meeting of May 30th [3] _____ and [4] _____. A formal complaint [5] _____ about the date of the meeting by Meg Taplock. It [6] _____ that in future meetings should not [7] _____ during exam time if possible.

After some debate about the choice of a replacement film for next year's programme, a vote [8] _____ and it [9] _____ by a majority decision to include Knife in the Water.

The meeting [10] _____ that nominations for club officers for next year should [11] _____ in the near future although it [12] _____ out that club rules do allow nominations to be made at the AGM. Votes of thanks to Carol Beynon and Brian Hill for their work during the year as Chair and Secretary respectively [13] _____ and [14] _____. In the absence of the Treasurer, the financial report [15] _____ over until the AGM.

It [16] _____ that the next committee meeting [17] _____ on Tuesday, October 10th at 6.00 pm

The Maniac Mile

The Maniac Mile is a race which takes place every year in the village of Meltham in Yorkshire in the north of England. This year, the race was held on June 30th at 7.30 pm.

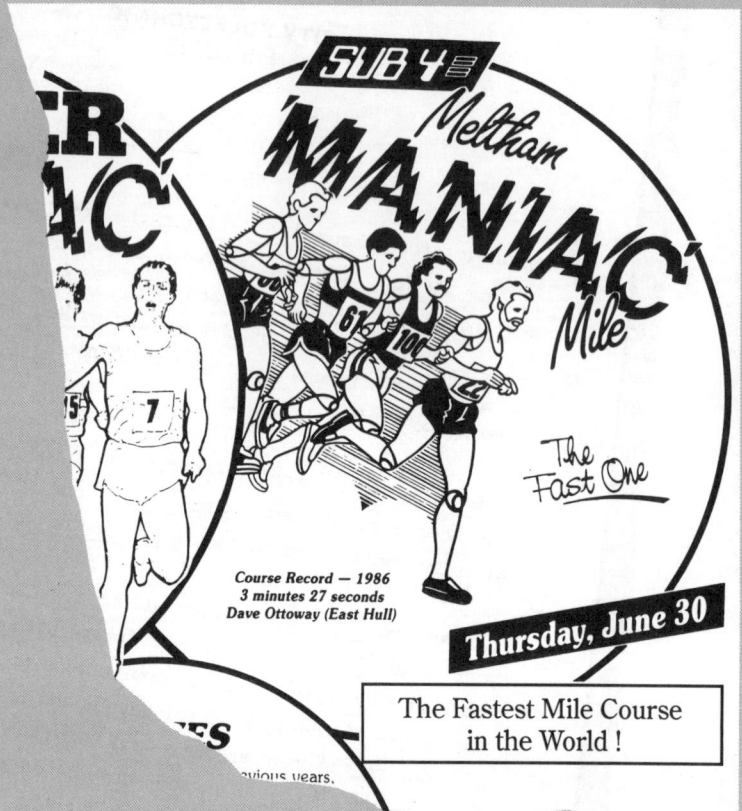

SUB 4

Meltham 'MANIAC' Mile

The Fast One

Course Record — 1986
3 minutes 27 seconds
Dave Ottoway (East Hull)

Thursday, June 30

The Fastest Mile Course in the World !

Pre-listening

1 Thinking about the topic

a) Is running or jogging popular in your country?

b) Why do you think this race is called the Maniac Mile?

c) What do you think would be the ideal weather conditions for a mile race?

d) In what ways do you think village life is different from life in a city?

2 Predicting language

Can you complete these sentences?

a) This race is a very popular _____.

b) Even if you don't win, it is fun to _____.

c) The previous best time for this race was not particularly fast. This year there are some very good runners so somebody will probably _____.

d) The time keeper will stop his watch when the winner's body _____.

e) The times of the other runners are recorded when their feet _____.

Extensive listening

1 Checking comprehension

a) In what way is the Maniac Mile different from a normal mile race?
b) What is the difference between the Murder Mile and the Maniac Mile?
c) What was the main aim of the serious athletes?
d) Were the weather conditions good for the runners?

2 Listening for gist

These sentences say something about the kind of people who took part in the race and the atmosphere of the occasion. Are the statements true or false?

a) It was a friendly, sociable occasion.
b) All the runners were serious athletes.
c) Men and women took part.
d) Most of the runners were concerned about their times.
e) Not everyone was enjoying the occasion.
f) Some people were taken away on stretchers.

Intensive listening

1 Focussing on vocabulary

Complete the gaps.

Organiser: This is an ¹_____ of my ²_____ race in as much as I started with what I call the murder mile. It's a mile uphill and I've just ³_____ it and this is downhill and this is the maniac.

Chris: And what about the ⁴_____? Because even walking I'm getting ⁵_____ walking up this.

Organiser: It's one in ten ⁶_____.

2 Understanding attitude or feelings

Look at the comments below. Which word in the box best describes the attitude of the speaker in each case?

a) *I bet you'll be glad when you're running down.*
b) *Yeah. I did three fifty-four last time.*
c) *No idea. Haven't a clue.*
d) *Not a chance. Not a chance.*
e) *I'll just be happy to get down.*
f) *She's just had her hair done.*
g) *Come on! You can do it.*
h) *It was bloody hard but I did it.*

realistic	encouraging	sympathetic	pleased
unambitious	joking	confident	unsure

3 Understanding humour

a) Did you understand the joke made by one of the runners at the end of the Unit?
Look at the *Answer key* to find other expressions with the same meaning.
b) Which other parts of the Unit did you find amusing?

VOCABULARY

maniac a person suffering from a mental disorder, a mad person
gradient the degree of slope or steepness
puffed out of breath (colloquial)
sadism pleasure in hurting other people
masochist a person who enjoys suffering or being hurt
stretcher a frame for carrying sick people, on which they can lie down
perm permanent wave; putting waves into straight hair that will last for several months
torrential violently rushing (water)
bolt a piece of metal used to hold parts of a machine together

Follow-up

1 Oral summary

Imagine you are a reporter for the local radio station in Yorkshire. Give your report of the Maniac Mile. You should include information about the following:

> background to the race   the village   the weather
> the spectators   the record   the winning time
> the band and the general atmosphere.

2 Interviewing other students

a) The Maniac Mile is a very popular local event in Yorkshire. Do you have any similar events in your home town which people can take part in or enjoy as spectators?

b) Ask another student about an event in his or her home town. Use these questions to help you.

- What is it called?
- When and how did it originate?
- What are the special features of the event?
- What is/are the aim/s?
- What kind of people take part?
- Are there many spectators?
- What else can you say about it?

c) Now tell the class about this event.

Study point

1 Using idioms

Look at the following words and expressions you have heard in this Unit.

What's the aim of it? To give everyone a run or to break records?
A bit of both.

I bet you'll be glad when you're running down.
No idea.
Haven't a clue.
Not a chance.
Here come the first bunch. ***Here come*** some more.
Come on! You can do it.
How was it?
How did you do?

Now use the words and expressions above to complete the following sentences.

a) Oh, you've finished your exams. _____?

b) He has _____ how much it costs. I don't know either.

c) We need another goal. _____ Liverpool!

d) Do you think they can beat Liverpool? No. _____.

e) Nice to see you back from your holiday. _____?

f) I don't know where she's gone and I _____ when she'll be back.

g) Q Why do you play so much tennis? Is it for the exercise or the social life?
    A _____.

h) I can hear the band playing. Look _____ the horses.

i) _____ he was angry when he saw the mess.

2 Word formation

Complete the boxes below with the appropriate adjective, verb, abstract noun or personal noun.

a)

Adjective	**Noun** (A)	**Noun** (P)
_____	sadism	_____
_____	_____	masochist

b)

Verb	**Noun** (A)	**Noun** (P)
_____	_____	organiser
originate	_____	_____
_____	participation	_____

Writing An article

Choose one of the following.
a) What aspects of the Meltham Maniac Mile do you think people in your country would find interesting?
   Write a short article about the event for a newspaper or magazine in your country.
b) Write an article for a British newspaper or magazine about a popular event in your country.

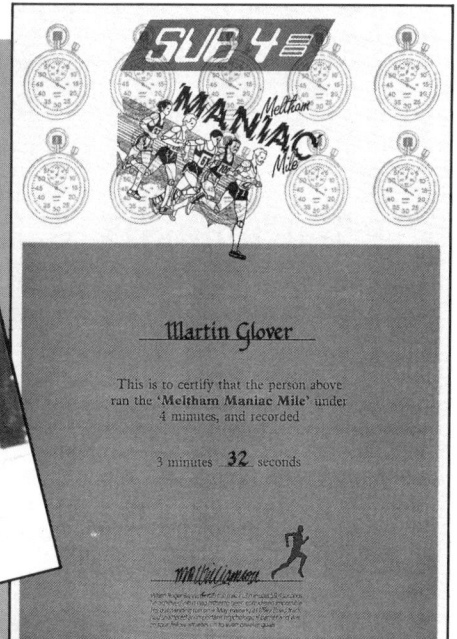

SUB 4
MANIAC Mile

Martin Glover

This is to certify that the person above ran the 'Meltham Maniac Mile' under 4 minutes, and recorded

3 minutes   32   seconds

Acid Rain

Adam Markham is the pollution campaign officer for Friends of the Earth, a British organisation working to promote a cleaner and safer environment.

Pre-listening

1 Predicting content

a) Have you heard of 'acid rain' before? What does the term acid rain suggest?

b) What would you like to know about acid rain? Write down three or four questions you would like to ask Adam Markham.

c) What aspects of acid rain do you think he will talk about?

d) Does your country suffer from pollution of any kind or have other environmental problems?

Extensive listening

1 Note-taking

It is impossible to write down everything the speaker says in a talk or lecture. Instead, you should aim to just get the 'skeleton' of the talk. These are some things that will help you.

● Use a large (A4) piece of paper.

● Arrange your notes clearly on the page.

- Underline or use capitals for the headings of the main sections of the talk.
- Number the sub-headings within each main section.
- Use abbreviations.
- Write clearly enough for you to understand your notes when you read them later.

a) Listen and take notes.
b) Compare your notes with another student's.

2 Evaluating the talk

a) How well can you answer these questions now?
   i)   What is acid rain?
   ii) How can acid rain be caused?
   iii) What kind of damage can it do?
   iv) Why is acid rain such a great problem for Britain?
   v)   What are the short term solutions?
   vi) What are the long term solutions?
b) How many of the questions you wrote down in the *Pre-listening* exercise 1b were answered?
c) What have you learned from the talk that you did not know before? Give one or more facts.

Intensive listening

1 Listening for specific details

Use these abbreviations to complete the sentences below. NO_x SO_2 HC O_3
a) _____ and _____ are primary pollutants.
b) _____ comes mainly from power stations.
c) _____ comes from _____ and power stations.
d) _____ is a secondary pollutant.
e) _____ + _____ + sunlight → _____.

2 Checking comprehension

Are these statements true or false?
a) Britain emits more sulphur dioxide than other countries in Western Europe.
b) The damage caused by sulphur dioxide from Britain only affects Scandinavia and other European countries.
c) Nations in the thirty percent club agreed to cut emissions by thirty percent by 1980.
d) A thirty percent cut in emissions over ten years will be enough.

3 Focussing on vocabulary

a) Complete the missing word in each gap.
   Unless we change society in this way, [1]_____ energy,
   [2]_____ our way of transport and now clean up our
   [3]_____ stations and individual cars, then we're
   [4]_____ to see more and worse [5]_____ effects from
   air [6]_____ and acid rain. We must act now.

b) Choose the correct meaning of these words as they are used here.

   i) *'conserve'* means $\left\{\begin{array}{l}\text{save}\\\text{create}\end{array}\right.$

   ii) *'rationalise'* means $\left\{\begin{array}{l}\text{find reasons for}\\\text{make more sensible and efficient}\end{array}\right.$

   iii) *'bound'* means $\left\{\begin{array}{l}\text{certain}\\\text{probable}\end{array}\right.$

Follow-up

1 Discussion

a) Adam says, *'We need a more efficient transport system which relies less on individuals' use of cars and more on good public transport.'*

In groups, discuss this statement with reference to a particular city you know well. Think about these questions.
- What kind of public transport system exists at present in the city? What are its advantages and disadvantages?
- Could individual drivers be persuaded to use public transport instead of their cars?

b) Make a plan to improve the transport system in the city. Take these factors into account.
- the wishes of private individuals
- the needs of particular groups
- the levels of pollution involved
- the cost to the government
- the cost to individuals

c) Summarise your group's discussion briefly for the rest of the class.

Study point

1 Lecture organisation

Good speakers try to help their audience follow the talk or lecture by indicating when they are moving from one point to another.

Think of as many different ways of completing these sentences as you can. Now look at the tapescript on page 81 to find out what the speaker said.

The introduction
The speaker will usually indicate which topics will be covered and in which order.
a) _____ acid rain.
b) _____ what acid rain is and why it's a problem.
c) _____ what we can do about it.

Starting a new section
This can be signalled by single words or by phrases.
d) _____ the chemicals involved.
e) _____ some of the solutions we should be looking to.

Indicating sub-sections to come
f) the chemicals involved. _____ These are sulphur dioxide, nitrogen oxides and ozone.
g) to stop this environmental catastrophe. _____ In the short term, we need to make immediate cuts.

Ending a section
h) a transport system which relies on a good public transport – er – network. _____ Unless we do that, unless we change society in this way.

Look at the *Answer key* to find other phrases that could be used.

2 Abbreviations

These abbreviations and symbols are useful when you are taking notes.

e.g.	for example	**viz**	namely	←	is caused by,
i.e.	that is	∴	therefore		results from
etc	etcetera, and so on	∵	because	>	greater than
N.B.	note particularly	→	causes, leads to	<	smaller than

Use the appropriate abbreviation or symbol from the list to complete these notes on the talk on acid rain.

a) damage to forests, lakes ____
b) ozone - secondary pollutant, ____ formed by combination of other prim. pollutants.
c) SO₂ in UK ____ pollution in Europe
d) angry with Brit. govt. ____ done nothing about problem
e) pollution in UK, ____ Wales and W. Scotland
f) Britain's SO₂ emission ____ anywhere in W. Europe

Writing Lecture notes

a) Two or three students should prepare a five minute talk about something they know very well. They can choose any topic. The other students must take notes while they are listening to the talk.
b) At the end of the talk, ask the speaker questions to clarify points made in the talk or to find out more about the topic.
c) Compare your notes with another student's.

TAPESCRIPT

UNIT ONE An American in London

Interviewer: What were the things in Britain that you found most strange when you first arrived?

Mathew: Well, the first thing is driving on the wrong side of the road . . . that would be the – that was very strange because you have this automatic reflex when you go out into the street to look one way and a couple of times I did that and I almost got hit by cars and bikes and all, you know. It's dangerous. It really is dangerous. And you have to teach yourself to look the other way.

Interviewer: Someone said that Britain and the United States are divided by a common language. Have you had any difficulties with the language here?

Mathew: Oh, yeah – tremendous amount of difficulty but I'm starting to pick it up now – all the lingo and slang and all those – but there's definitely a difference.

Interviewer: Can you give me any examples?

Mathew: Well, the big – I'd say some of the biggest ones would be the word 'queue' which means in America 'line'. I never heard the word 'queue' before. Um – what you call 'chips', I call 'French fries'. I never heard them called 'chips'. Um – there's so many – um – words that are different. Ah – 'crisps' which mean 'potato chips'. Yeah, that's – we call them 'potato chips' or 'chips' in America. You call them 'crisps' here. So when I heard the word 'chips', I was thinking of 'crisps' and not French fri – you know – it's very confusing but – um – but just some of the expressions like – er – 'mate' you know and 'love'. Those – you know – they're funny. You don't hear them. You don't hear them in America.

Interviewer: What about with young people – with people your own age – I mean, do you notice differences there?

Mathew: I do notice some differences – er – I think – ah – I think the younger people in Britain are – they seem to be – much more radical than the younger people in the United States. I noticed that. Ah – the dress is different. You see a lot of – I see a lot of males here with earrings in one of their – in one of their ears. You don't see that in America that much. Somet – maybe here and there, but not, not like you see it here. Ah – so many of the young people wear black – clothing – you know. I don't – you don't see the other colours. At home you see all different types of bright colours – and in England you see so much black. Especially on the women.

Interviewer: You don't like that?

Mathew: Not really. It's just my own preference. I like – I'd rather see different colours here and there – not all – not all one colour. Everyone looks like Madonna.

Interviewer: When you say 'radical' – do you – are you just thinking of clothes or of anything else?

Mathew: Um – No, I think – er – radical as in going against the norms – could you say? Not only in clothing but I think in politics too whereas in America – er – you don't find that as much. Oh, also, another difference is the young – er – the younger people are — they're more politically aware on a larger level. See a lot of the – a lot of the Americans – they're aware of – er – government of the United States and maybe a few other countries but not as many countries in Europe or they just have a vague understanding of how those other countries are run – not as widespread. Whereas here, I think that they – er – the kids get to know about how different countries are run at a much younger level and they know all

about the United States and how it's run.

Interviewer: What do you think the reasons are for that?

Mathew: Um – that's a good question – um – well, I think that the reasons are – just because of the Press. You hear so much about America here that people are – they're into it – they want to know what it's about and how it's run. And so many of our policies in America affect Britain that they want to understand how policies are made and all that and seeing that that doesn't work on the other level like Britain's policies don't – I mean, they can affect us, but not to as great an extent and therefore you don't hear as much about Britain and people don't know as much about it.

UNIT TWO Visiting India

Liz: Well, I'm planning a trip. Now you've just been to India. I know you've been to India, Julia. This is where I'm thinking of going – um –

Julia: You lucky girl. I wish I could go again.

Liz: Now whereabouts would you suggest that – is the best part to go?

Marsha: Well, there's only one part that I've been to and that's up in the north. Most of the time I was in Kashmir, in Srinagar. And Julia, you were – you were in the same place?

Julia: I was in Srinagar too. Yes.

Liz: I know you went like a month ago.

Marsha: Yeah.

Liz: Um – so – that was in June July. When – when did you go?

Julia: I went in the – over the Christmas period in eighty three four.

Liz: Right. And if – if – um – I went to the northern part that both of you recommend and have been to – is the weather greatly different – um – near Christmas and – ?

Marsha: Yes. It gets quite cold there in the winter. It's very cold there in the winter.

Julia: Yes. Extremely cold.

Liz: What about – but if you go in the summer – do you – I mean – ?

Marsha: Yes. It's quite nice in the summer because when it's really hot on the plain up in Srinagar it's in the hills and that's where people go to get away from the heat of places like Delhi.

Liz: What about the food – did you – ?

Julia/Marsha: Oh, it was wonderful food.

Liz: But – um – did you – I mean people always think India – oh god – you know – it's how hot – you have to eat the curries very hot because that's – ?

Marsha: Never had a hot curry.

Julia: No. No.

Marsha: They were all perfectly (possible to eat)

Julia: Very edible, yeah.

Liz: Oh, right.

Marsha: And Kashmiri food is very good and very mild. One of the best things I had was pumpkin in a yoghurt sauce.

Julia: Their vegetables are beautiful. They grow an awful lot of them. Did you see a lot of them growing? Greens? Spinach?

Marsha: Spinach was in season. Oh – I love the pureed spinach.

Julia: Mm.

Liz: If you had – knew somebody who was going just for a week what were – how would you advise them to spend their – um – I mean – what things are absolutely

unmissable – um – around that area?
Julia: Well, we – we were told –
Liz: You only had four days, didn't you?
Julia: Yes, we were only there for four days but we packed the four days with trips and sightseeing trips. And we went to see Pahalgam which was a wonderful trip. Just a little mountain town nestling in the foot of the Himalayas. But it was about a hundred kilometres away from Srinagar. But the scenery was just out of this world.
Marsha: There's – oh, there's – there's a museum which is in what was the Maharajah's palace.
Julia: That's well worth a visit. The museum.
Marsha: Yes.
Liz: What about – didn't you say something about – before – about some gardens?
Julia/Marsha: Oh, the gardens. Yes.
Marsha: There are dozens of Mogul gardens. We –
Liz: What are the moguls?
Julia: Shalimar. Oh, mogul.
Marsha: Mogul. That was from the Mogul period. That was — what — eighteenth century?
Julia: Yes.
Marsha: The Mogul emperors built these gardens and they have a –
Julia: Very formal.
Marsha: Yes. There's a pattern to all of them. With – there's a – they're on several levels – terraces. They're terraced.
Julia: Yes.
Marsha: And there's a water channel going through the middle.
Julia: And lots of fountains.
Marsha: Mm.
Julia: And very formal flower beds.
Marsha: And –
Julia: And huge trees.
Liz: What about – um – sort of bargains that you should look out for to – to –?
Julia/Marsha: Oh, well. Kashmir. Everything.
Julia: Silk.
Liz: Oh.
Julia: We went into a silk – er – shop. And inside it was just a glimmer of silk of every colour you could think of. It was absolutely beautiful.
Liz: And did you get tempted to bring back things you couldn't possibly carry or – ?
Julia/Marsha: Oh, yes.
Marsha: I brought back a bedspread. Cotton. Quilted. But beautifully – but beautiful soft cotton and – and so much handwork done.
Julia: I'll tell you another thing –
Marsha: Honey.
Julia: – I bought and couldn't bring back with me.
Liz: Honey.
Marsha: Mm. Wonderful honey in Kashmir.
Julia: I bought a rug. A lovely Kashmiri rug. They have factories and rug shops all over the place, don't they?
Marsha: Mm.
Julia: I've thought of something else which is well worth buying if you buy small pieces and that's wood carvings. Um – cigarette boxes and bowls. Er – well worth looking at.
Liz: Are they the sort of things that you see sometimes with mother-of-pearl inlaid? Do you know – ?
Julia: I didn't see any like that. This was just pure maple from the maple trees around the place. But in Delhi there was a lot of wood carving with little mother-of-pearl inlay.

Marsha: The other thing that Kashmir is famous for is the papier maché.
Julia: Oh, yes.
Marsha: Beautiful little boxes and – and –
Julia: Er – what else?
Marsha: Trays.
Julia: Trays. Yes. Er – cocktail mats in their own box all to match. Um – they use gold leaf for painting some of those, don't they?
Marsha: Yes.
Julia: And you can actually watch it being done by . . . .

UNIT THREE   Before Breakfast

Announcer: Ladies and gentlemen, this is the last call for breakfast. The dining car is located towards the rear of the train. Last call for breakfast.

Tom: Um. The full English breakfast, please.
Waiter: Yes sir. Tea or coffee?
Tom: Um. Tea, please. No, coffee. Oh. No, I'd better have tea.
Waiter: What's it to be then?
Tom: Tea. I'm trying to cut out coffee. I drink far too much of it.
Waiter: Right you are, sir. Full English breakfast. With tea.
Tom: Coffee.
Waiter: But you said –
Tom: No. I've changed my mind. Well, you only live once.
Waiter: As you wish, sir.

Joanna: Excuse me. Is this seat free?
Tom: Yes.
Joanna: Can I sit down then?
Tom: You can if you can bend your knees.
Joanna: Why shouldn't I be able to bend my knees? Oh, yes, I see. It was a joke.
Tom: Afraid so. Are you going to sit down?
Joanna: Thank you.
Tom: The dining car isn't very crowded this morning.
Joanna: Perhaps not many people like to eat breakfast any more. Breakfast has been getting a bad press lately. All that cholesterol. Heart disease and that sort of thing.
Waiter: Yes, miss?
Joanna: Full English breakfast, please. With coffee. I'd like the coffee straightaway, please.
Waiter: It'll be along shortly.
Joanna: Good. I love coffee. I couldn't live without it.
Tom: Well, there's no need to.
Joanna: I suppose you think it's strange.
Tom: Oh, not at all. I drink a lot of coffee myself.
Joanna: No. I mean strange about me wanting to sit here, next to you, when there are two empty tables and lots of spare places.
Tom: I hadn't really noticed.
Joanna: Yes, you did. It was the first thing you said when I sat down.
Tom: I can't remember what I said. I was just making conversation.
Joanna: You said the dining car wasn't crowded.
Tom: Well, it wasn't. It isn't. I didn't mean to imply anything.
Joanna: Perhaps you didn't mean to, but you did.
Waiter: Coffee for both?
Tom: Yes, please.
Waiter: Black or white?

Joanna: } White.
Tom: } White.
Joanna: Snap!
Tom: Yes.
Joanna: Thank you.
Tom: Thanks.
Joanna: You don't recognise me, do you?
Tom: Yes, I do.
Joanna: Honestly?
Tom: Yes. You're the girl who came and sat down at this table a couple of minutes ago.
Joanna: You know that's not what I meant. Don't you recognise me from before? From a long time ago.
Tom: Now you come to mention it –
Joanna: Yes?
Tom: And now that I look at you more closely –
Joanna: Yes?
Tom: I don't believe I've ever seen you before in my life.
Joanna: Well, then how is it that I know your name?
Tom: I'm not aware that you do know my name.
Joanna: Well, I do. Tom.
Tom: Well, I have to admit that you do know my name. My first name, anyway.
Joanna: I only ever knew your first name. I'm Joanna.
Tom: Joanna.
Joanna: Well, doesn't the name ring a bell?
Tom: Not at all.
Joanna: But we were in love.
Tom: I've never been in love.
Joanna: Well, then you were lying to me. You declared your undying passion.
Tom: Look. This is getting embarrassing. The next thing you're going to tell me is that we're married.
Joanna: You did propose to me, but I turned you down.
Tom: Sensible girl.
Joanna: I said we were too young to marry.
Tom: When did all this happen?
Joanna: Seven years ago. Seven years and three months, to be exact.
Tom: I was only fourteen then.
Joanna: I was twelve.
Tom: We were too young to marry. You were absolutely right to turn me down.
Joanna: Yes, I was right. All the same, I've regretted it ever since. It's been the day I've remembered all my life. That day in Cornwall when we met at the top of Tintagel Castle and you bought me a cream tea. And when we said goodbye, you gave me a peck on the cheek.
Tom: You're joking, aren't you? Or playing some kind of silly game? You're not from one of those TV shows, are you?
Joanna: Oh, Tom. Of course not.
Tom: Then it's all a case of mistaken identity. As it happens, I did once spend a holiday in Tintagel and I do remember having a cream tea. But I have absolutely no recollection of you.
Joanna: I had pigtails.
Tom: I'm sure I was with my parents.
Joanna: I find it hard to believe that an event so important in my life could have had so little meaning in yours.
Tom: Obviously this event, if it actually happened, made no impression on me. You made no impression on me.
Joanna: That's very hurtful.
Tom: I'm being honest with you.
Joanna: Well, you forgot me very quickly. You promised to write and so did I. Well, I waited for you to write first because I wasn't quite sure what to say.

Tom: So you're not suddenly going to confront me with a letter in my handwriting.
Joanna: You never wrote. I assumed you'd lost my address.
Tom: Clearly, this romance was never meant to be.
Joanna: Well, I'm glad now. All these years later, I discover that I don't like you very much.
Tom: You hardly know me.
Joanna: You've become pompous and unkind. I don't want to talk to you any more.
Tom: Oh, don't – don't go.
Joanna: Why shouldn't I?
Tom: You've ordered breakfast.
Joanna: Well, I'll sit at another table. Anyway, I'm not hungry.
Tom: Please, sit down.
Joanna: There doesn't seem to be much point.
Tom: Please.
Joanna: Oh, all right.
Tom: You see, Joanna, this morning we started off on the wrong foot. I've got a feeling that if we start off as if we've only just met, things might turn out differently.
Joanna: Well, you could be right.
Tom: Right then. Well, we'd better introduce ourselves. I'm Tom Watkins.
Joanna: I'm Joanna Hayes.
Tom: How do you do?
Joanna: How do you do?
Tom: Do you know. I think we might get to like each other quite a bit. Now that we've met as strangers.

UNIT FOUR Looking Back

Interviewer: Peter, Barbara and John have very different family backgrounds but they all have happy memories of childhood.
Peter: We lived in a one-bedroom flat and there was me and my older sister and my younger brother and my parents all had the same bedroom. My mother used to take us down to the Thames near Tower Bridge and there was then – I don't know if there still is – but there was a bit of beach. When the tide was out, you could actually go down some steps onto the sand there. I mean I imagine now it's pretty mucky but at the time it was – it was wonderful being able to go to the – what we thought was the seaside in the middle 'of London. No – those were lovely times actually – watching the boats go by. Smashing.
Barbara: There was always parties. Um – birthday parties. There was four of us and my aunts – they had children – so whenever it was anyone's birthday we all had a party. Of course, my mum – she used to make lovely cakes. And we was always round someone's house sort of playing and laughing. Quite – I mean it was all good fun when we was kids. When I was bridesmaid, I had this gorgeous dress on – or so I thought – it was all pink and rosebuds. And this great big – I don't know if it was a limousine or something – come for me and me brother. And we was sitting in the back and I was waving like the Queen and everyone was looking. I thought it was fantastic. I think that's got to be one of the highlights – or so I thought – of my life – at the time. I mean – It was just great.
John: Certainly one of the happiest memories of my childhood was just getting on a bike with a packet of sandwiches and a bottle of lemonade and going off for the day and just discovering the – the wonderful

countryside that I was lucky enough to be surrounded by. I was a very solitary sort of child. I suppose being an only child living in a very remote village − er − contributed to this. Er − I was a solitary child. I enjoyed my own company, I suppose. And I was very keen on nature. I managed to acquire an old tatty pair of binoculars and used to go and sit on top of hills and look at birds and things.

Interviewer: They are very lucky to have such good experiences to remember. But not even the happiest childhood is perfect. There are always some anxieties and fears.

Peter: Yes, when I was quite little I was very frightened of the dark. Um − and particularly − I don't know what it was or where I'd got it − got it from − but I was − I was afraid of things coming out of the wall.

Barbara: I just had nightmares. Me mum took me to the doctor because I just could not sleep. I was frightened to close me eyes in case I'd die. It was awful.

John: There was a lot of bullying at the school I went to. It was mostly physical violence really − it was carting young lads off behind the bike sheds and thumping them. Or it was − they'd go as far as stealing their pocket money. And − quite unpleasant really.

Interviewer: There are always some particular occasions which stay in our minds. John remembers the day he gave his grandmother a shock and Peter tells a sad story about a pet.

John: My grandmother used to spend three months of the year with us − my maternal grandmother − who I loved dearly. And I remember one day when she was visiting − um − she was coming up the front garden path and I was perched on my bedroom window sill which overlooked the front garden path deciding that I wanted to be a parachutist. And I had my father's umbrella and I leapt off this window sill with my father's umbrella open and landed in front of my grandmother and I think the poor old dear had a − almost a premature heart attack. She did live to be nearly ninety so it didn't do her too much harm.

Peter: Mostly we used to have budgies. Um − oh − well − the saddest thing that happened to one of our budgies was the time when it was playing on the floor with its toys. We used to let it out of its cage and we put its little toys − you know the sort of thing that they knock over and that stands up again − and we had those on the floor. And the budgie was − you know − hopping around on the floor playing with these toys right near the settee and my father was sitting on the settee or sort of lying on the settee with his legs up and he put his legs down to get up and go somewhere − er − he put his feet down on the floor to go somewhere and he trod on the budgie. And I mean you can imagine the absolute scenes of mayhem. Um − I mean we were − we were totally distraught. And I − oh − it was awful. I mean I remember picking up the budgie and I was holding it in my hands when it died. You know − I mean − it was obviously fairly mangled by my father. And my poor father. I mean he was − you know − he felt terrible about it. He didn't know what to do. I mean − there wasn't anything he could do really. But − oh dear − that was I think probably one of the most ghastly moments in my childhood.

UNIT FIVE   The Long Essay

Tutor: You have experience with this age group in
Selvi: I have

Tutor: in Singapore or −?
Selvi: In Malaysia.
Tutor: In Mal − in other parts of Malaysia. Right. When you were teaching this age group, were they bilingual?
Selvi: They were bilingual.
Tutor: Um − were they in English medium schools?
Selvi: English medium schools.
Tutor: Ah − right. Well, that's very useful experience, isn't it? Yes. And you were teaching English, were you?
Selvi: Yes. English and other subjects.
Tutor: Mm.
Selvi: But they were in English.
Tutor: Right. So you were like a form teacher
Selvi: right
Tutor: teaching the whole range of subjects. Well that's very, very useful background for this project, I think. Um − but you've also got here . . . short stories and poems for practising phonetics.
Selvi: Well − actually − what − what I intended was this − this communicative − er − materials
Tutor: mm
Selvi: You know − in the form of short stories
Tutor: yes
Selvi: You see − and poems.
Tutor: Yes. Poems . . . you mean poems that have been published that you
Selvi: no
Tutor: that you can use with them − you want them to write poems?
Selvi: No. I mean through my poems the poems that I'm going to write.
Tutor: You're going to write poems. Oh, that sounds wonderful. What − simple poems?
Selvi: Simple poems so that the children would find it, you know, like a sing-song.
Tutor: Um − I think what we need actually is a slightly more specific plan
Selvi: right
Tutor: than this one. Shall we see if we can make a plan? Using a topic-based approach − um − to the teaching of English as a second language − um − to seven to eleven year-old bilingual children. Um − So we take that as the title − then probably − now − there are lots of different things here. You − you need some kind of section that discusses − Now − first of all you want to talk about context don't you? And you want − um − let's say London and Malaysia just to discuss what we said − um − can the materials be universal? And then you want something on criteria
Selvi: mm
Tutor: for designing these. Now what − let's just list the ones we've mentioned. Can we go through them? What have we got here? Motivation. So we're thinking of seven to eleven year-olds. Motivation. What are the important ones, do you think? Multi-cultural − um − communicative − um − what else have we said? Cross-curricular. Those are the four main ones, aren't they? Oh − integrated skills.
Selvi: Oh, yes
Tutor: Right. Integrated skills. And when you're discussing those criteria, you can mention, you can bring in − relate it to poems, stories − um − and tasks that they do. And then you − you actually want your materials. So you need to choose a topic
Selvi: materials topic
Tutor: where you can put these together. And then you want to − after you've actually presented the materials − you want some detailed comments on different parts of them. How does that sound?

Selvi: Very, very impressive. Very good.

Tutor: Does that make sense to you − if we put it like that? So we've really taken all of those things and just slightly rearranged them. Okay? I think that sounds very, very interesting.

UNIT SIX A Sense of Humour

Sandy: I do know again a true story of which in a way epitomises the Irish − um − sense of humour. Although in fact it wasn't even really, in this particular instance, it wasn't said as a witty remark. But it was a friend of mine who was working in the south of Ireland and he was driving along a lane and he turned a corner and there was a herd of pigs with a swineherd being driven on foot along this lane. And it was a very narrow road and he thought, 'Well, I'm completely stymied. I mean, there's no way I'm going to get past a herd of pigs.' So he got out of his car and started to talk to the swineherd. And he said, 'How far are you taking the pigs?', wanting to find out how long he was going to be behind this lot. And the swineherd said, 'Oh, sure, they're going to County Cork.' And this friend of mine said, 'But that's a very long way. It's fifteen miles. Wouldn't it be better to take them by lorry?' And the swineherd said, 'Well, I suppose when you say it, it would be. But then if you think about it, what's time to pigs?' Which is quin −

Friend: That's lovely though.

Sandy: That's − that really is true and it's quintessentially Irish as well. 'Cause I remember also working in the south of Ireland. I had a taxi driver once and it was in the end of the summer and I said, 'It must be very quiet here in the winter. You know, what do you do for business? I mean there are no tourists and −' He said, 'Oh, well, the winter's very quiet,' he said, 'but I don't drive a taxi in the winter. I drive the hearse.' And I said, 'Oh I see.' And he said, 'Well, you see, unlike tourism, that business is very quiet in the summer, but the winter's lovely. They die like flies.'

Friend: Is that is that typically Irish?

Sandy: It is. Yes. It really is. They have a − they have a wonderful sense of the absurd and the macabre. It's like − I mean that is slightly macabre.

Sandy: I don't know about a British sense of humour. I think there are regional senses of humour and they're all very different. I think − um − I mean I think that's one of the problems with humour in Great Britain − is that things that strike people as very funny in − ah − Scotland, for example, don't particularly strike − wouldn't strike the Irish as particularly funny because they're nearly all plays on words using sometimes dialect − um − usages. Er − I mean the one that we were talking about which is based on − um − well, it's based on several things. You have to know that there's a show called 'No, No, Nannette' − um − It's a musical, a musical comedy. It was written in the twenties, I think, or maybe a bit before even. Um − and that in Scotland − er − if you want to say − if you're speaking Scots dialect and you want to say 'I am not going' you would say 'I'm no going.' The 'not' becomes 'no'. The 't' gets dropped and it becomes 'no'. But if you're Scottish you know very clearly the differentiation between the usages of the word 'no'. Um − like 'He's no coming today' − 'He's not coming today'. Um − and this actually is a true st − this really did happen. Er − a person who was singing with an opera company, who were on tour in Edinburgh,

went into a flower shop to buy some flowers for somebody who was going on − an understudy, I think − who was going on to do the performance that night. And bought a bunch of flowers and this very sweet little Edinburgh lady who served him with his flowers − after he'd paid − she said, 'Excuse me. Are you in show business?'. And he said, 'Yes. I am, actually.' And she said, 'Aha. I thought so. You can always tell.' And he said, 'Oh, really.' And she said, 'Oh yes, of course. I used to be in show business myself.' And he said, 'Oh, really.' And she said, 'Oh, yes. I was in No No Nannette.' And he looked completely blank because he'd never heard of it. And she looked at him and said, 'Do you no know No No Nannette?' which is a classic really but you do have to know the conditions before it's really as funny as it − as it is −

Friend: I think it's wonderful.

Friend: But, you see, we all find that's funny even though we're not Scottish.

Sandy: Yes, but it has to be explained. I mean −

Friend: No, but −

Sandy: A lot of − a lot of British people know that in Scotland the word 'not' becomes 'no'. You know, 'Will ye no come back again?' In the song. Yes, there are certain basic − Things are funny or not. You know.

Friend: Or no.

Sandy: Or no. Yes.

UNIT SEVEN A Card Trick

Bert: Hold out your hand. I'm going to lay one card on your hand. Okay. Now let's just think about what's happened. You're thinking of a card. I didn't see the card. I didn't touch the card. I couldn't know what the card was. What is the card that you're thinking of?

Interviewer: Ace of hearts.

Bert: Turn that card over and tell us what it is.

Interviewer: Oh. It's the ace of hearts. That's wonderful. How did you do it?

Bert: Well, I'm now going to break all the rules of magic and tell you how I did that.

Interviewer: And tell me the secret.

Bert: Okay. It's a very simple trick to do. First of all, you need two things. You need a pack of cards and you need a person to show the trick to. Right and you are now the magician, and you say to me, 'Please shuffle the cards.'

Interviewer: Okay. Right. Please would you shuffle the cards.

Bert: I would. Okay. I've shuffled the cards. Now I give them back to you.

Interviewer: Right.

Bert: Now at this moment, the most important part of the trick is about to happen, but I − I'm the audience − I mustn't know anything about it. You have to look at the bottom card of the pack and remember what it is. You have to do that secretly so that it's not obvious. That was pretty obvious − the way you did it just then.

Interviewer: Yes. Well, I'm not very good at this.

Bert: A good way to do it is to take the cards and pretend to be squaring them up after the person has shuffled them. You can tap them on the table to square them up. And that's a good way because that gives you a very natural way of looking at the bottom card. So you do that.

Interviewer: Okay. I'll have to practise that, but I've seen it now.

Bert: And you've remembered what it is.

Interviewer: I remember what it is.

Bert: You must remember. If you forget what that card is, you can't do the trick and you look a right idiot. Okay. Now you say to me, 'Please cut the cards.'

Interviewer: Okay. So please cut the cards.

Bert: Okay. I'm cutting the cards – that's to say I'm taking off about half the pack – so I'm leaving you, the magician, with the bottom half and I've got the top half.

Interviewer: Okay.

Bert: Now you say to me, 'Please look at the top card of the ones that I am holding.'

Interviewer: Okay. So please look at the top card of the ones I'm holding.

Bert: Okay. That's the card that was in the very middle of the pack. And I'm looking at it.

Interviewer And remember that card.

Bert: That's very important. You must say, 'Please remember the card.' Okay. I'm looking at it. I'm going to remember what it is.

Interviewer: And now please put your card on the top of the cards you are holding.

Bert: Okay. I'm putting it back on what was the very top of the pack of cards. I'm putting it back on the top of the half that I'm holding.

Interviewer: Mm.

Bert: There it goes.

Interviewer: Okay.

Bert: Now you are going to put your half of the pack – the magician's half – on top of my half.

Interviewer: Right.

Bert: Now that looks as though what you've done is buried my card right in the middle of the pack but what you've really done is put the card that you're remembering right next to my card. It means that any time you want you can find my card by finding your card. And that's what you've got to do now.

Interviewer: All right. And this is the moment where I ask you to think very hard of the card.

Bert: This is the moment when the acting comes in.

Interviewer: Right.

Bert: You've got to take my mind away from what you're doing. Okay. I'm thinking of my card.

Interviewer: Okay. Concentrate, please.

Bert: I'm concentrating like mad.

Interviewer: I can only find it if you think very very hard.

Bert: That's very good. You're learning very quickly. Yes, I'm thinking very hard of my card. And while I'm thinking, what you're doing – what the magician is doing – is looking for the card that you're remembering.

Interviewer: Right. Now I've found the card that I saw but – so your card must be next to it – but will it be above my card or below?

Bert: No. It'll be the one below the card you're remembering because remember what you did – you took your half of the pack and put it on top of my half. So your card that you're secretly remembering is on top of the card that I took.

Interviewer: Okay.

Bert: So now you know what my card is.

Interviewer: Right. I think I've done this correctly. And this should be your card. Now, it was a lucky number.

Bert: Yes, I think that's true. It was a lucky number.

Interviewer: Number seven.

Bert: Number seven – that's amazing.

Interviewer: And it was the seven of diamonds.

Bert: It was the seven of diamonds. And you've put a card on my hand and I turn it over and it's the seven of diamonds. That's an amazing trick. How did you do it?

Interviewer: It's a secret. I couldn't possibly tell you.

UNIT EIGHT   The Macbeth Ordeal

Gerry: The world of the theatre is full of superstitions. Most, if not all, actors subscribe to them. The commonest superstition concerns Shakespeare's play 'Macbeth'. It's considered to be extremely unlucky. Indeed, it's even unlucky to quote lines from it or to mention it by name. When they have to talk about it, people in the theatrical profession refer to it as 'the Scottish play'. Nevertheless, when I was offered the title role, I jumped at the chance of playing it despite the warnings of my superstitious girlfriend.

Emma: Honestly, Gerry, you must be mad. Just remember the history of deaths and disasters connected with that play.

Gerry: Nonsense. I bet there've been some very happy productions of the Scottish play.

Emma: You're making a big mistake. I have premonitions of disaster already. Gerry, you're not listening!

Gerry: Yes, I am.

Emma: You were looking in the mirror.

Gerry: I was imagining myself with a beard.

Emma: You're not going to grow a beard.

Gerry: Macbeth should have a beard.

Emma: Well, you don't have to grow one. You could stick one on.

Gerry: If the play is as unlucky as you insist, the beard would come unstuck. Probably in the middle of a big speech.

Emma: I wouldn't like you with a beard.

Gerry: Emma, what are you trying to say?

Emma: I'm telling you not to grow a beard.

Gerry: I'm going to.

Emma: Well, on your own head be it.

Gerry: On my own chin, you mean, don't you?

Emma: Ha, ha. Most hilarious.

Gerry: Three weeks later I had a beard but no longer had a girlfriend. The break up of our relationship had nothing to do with the bad luck associated with the play. We'd spent a lot of our time quarrelling. We had so little in common that quarrelling was a way of passing the time. My beard, however, was a great success, with a considerable amount of red in it. Highly appropriate for a Scottish king. So complete with two old suitcases and one new beard, I set out for Inverness. I forgot to say – the Scottish play was to be performed in Scotland! It's a long journey from London at the best of times, but that day was 'one of those days'. The train left Kings Cross on time but after that there was an endless series of delays. I finally arrived at Inverness at one o'clock in the morning, three hours late. I'd been travelling for nearly twelve hours. Of course, it was all highly predictable. I shouldn't have travelled on a Sunday because that's when they do all the engineering works on the line. There were no buses at that time of night so I had to take a taxi to Alison's. She was in charge of publicity at the theatre and I was going to stay with her and her husband at their cottage. I apologised for arriving so late and Alison led me upstairs to my room. I was to sleep in the attic.

Alison: It's only a small room but I'm sure you'll be comfortable and warm. And this is a quiet area, so you won't be disturbed when you're learning your lines.

Gerry: Oh, you've got a cat.

Alison: We've got three. Bushytail, Ragtag and Emerald the kitten. That little fellow is Bushytail.

Gerry: Hullo, Bushytail.

I didn't like to mention it, but I have a problem with cats. It's not that I don't like them. Although, I'm not crazy about them. It's just that unfortunately most cats affect my chest and give me bad attacks of asthma. I crossed my fingers and hoped that I'd be lucky with these cats. Unfortunately, I wasn't. Shortly after two thirty, I woke up gasping for breath. The cats had probably been playing in the bedclothes. I dressed as fast as I could and left a note for Alison to explain. Then I went out into the chilly November night, looking for somewhere else to stay. There was bound to be a hotel open somewhere – even in Inverness. I didn't care about the price, I just wanted a good sleep. As I walked towards the centre of town, it began to rain. The streets were deserted. The only sign of life was a police car which I saw disappearing up the road. I could see what looked like a hotel ahead so I carried on walking. It was called the Hibernian Hotel. The glass-fronted doors were locked, so I rang the bell.

All the lights are on. There must be someone on duty. At long last, a middle-aged man appeared. He opened the door, introduced himself as the manager and asked me what I wanted. There was something strange about the way he spoke, but I was relieved to hear that they did have a vacancy. So I filled in the registration form and told him my story – about the cats and my asthma. He didn't seem to find it very convincing and just stood there staring at me. I suppose I must have looked rather odd myself. Suddenly, there was a scream. I turned round and saw a woman who I assumed to be the manager's wife. Behind her was a policeman.

Woman: That's him. That's him, officer. A thousand pounds. He took a thousand pounds. It's that beard, you see.

Gerry: I could say nothing in defence of my beard because by this time the manager had grabbed me by the throat. I think he would have strangled me if the policeman hadn't sprung to my rescue and pulled him away.

Policeman: That's all right, Sir. We'll deal with this. Now, young man, I think you have some questions to answer.

Gerry: As I rubbed my neck and checked that my beard was still attached to my face, one thing became clear – there would be no sleep for me that night.

UNIT NINE Office Life

Anne: Good afternoon. Can I speak to Geoff Corbett? Ah. It's Anne Biggs. Can you phone me? Anne Biggs, extension three one three six. Um. No. I want to book some orders in and I've got a quote. Okay? Thank you very much. Bye bye.

Joanna: Well, I think this is fairly typical of a big office – um – you're going to have a lot of girls who're going to be spending time answering telephone calls. A lot of the calls are going to be inter-departmental calls.

Kathy: Oh, I was trying to get hold of Julie. Is she there? Oh, Julie, just a moment, please. Julie.

Julie: Yes.

Kathy: Sorry. It's Kathy here. Um – those cassettes that we're doing for you – the – er

Julie: Yes.

Kathy: Could you give me the account code number to which they're to be charged?

Julie: Yes. Er – just a second.

Kathy: Thank you.

Julie: Hullo.

Kathy: Yes.

Julie: Right. It's seven four.

Kathy: Seven four.

Julie: Six oh.

Kathy: Six oh.

Julie: Oh five.

Kathy: Oh five.

Julie: Oh oh.

Kathy: Oh oh. Is there anything before that? Is there another –

Julie: The divisional code is –

Kathy: Yes.

Julie: Oh – mm – it's a funny one. It's changed. Hang on a minute.

Julie: Four. W – oh – nine.

Kathy: Four. W – oh – nine.

Julie: Yes.

Kathy: Lovely. Thanks very much. Bye.

Julie: Bye.

Kathy: Bye bye.

Joanna: I think if you're going to be good working on the telephone you have to have an enormous amount of patience particularly if you're dealing with the public because there are going to be lots of queries which to you seem quite ridiculous – um – but to outsiders are terribly important.

Lyn: Hullo. I'm afraid I don't know where he is at the moment. May I take a message?

Caller: Um – could you – um – do you know when he's likely to – he is around, is he?

Lyn: He is around today, yes, but he's not actually in his office at the moment.

Caller: Um. Could you just tell him Willy Gaminara phoned?

Lyn: Willy Gaminara. Certainly.

Peter: It's all right. I'll speak to him now.

Lyn: Just one moment.

Peter: Willy. Oh, hi, Willy. It's Peter Marsh. Willy, I'm sorry about that. . . . . .

Joanna: Yes – I think if you work as a private secretary, you really have to be almost a buffer between the public and your boss. And you have to be able to judge how important the calls are, how important they're going to be to him, how busy he is and whether he wants to talk to the person then or whether you can just take a message and deliver it to him later. Working in an office, part of the routine is dealing with invoices and today we did have a particular problem. It was something to do with a freelance worker I'm not sure exactly what the problem was but no doubt we'll sort it out.

Kay: Hullo. Is that Vera? Oh, can you hang on a sec? Sorry. Hullo, Vera. Sorry about that. It's Kay. Um – we've got some actors' payments here. The invoices are in front of me. And – um – the copy that comes over from you, on the bottom where you've got the total net earnings, the national insurance, the employee's contribution etcetera.

Vera: Mm.

Kay: Um – there's – there seems to be a differing figure. There's – um – there's a figure of – where the total gross earnings is sixty-nine pounds.

Vera: Yeah.

Kay: and then eleven pounds ten pence in overtime.

Vera: In overtime?

Kay: Yeah. And that is actually detailed on the invoice and – you know the actual cheque was made out for the right amount.

Vera: Yeah.

Kay: The only thing that we can't figure out is your figure at the very bottom of the page which says seventy-three pound eighty-six which is only the actual payment of sixty-nine pound and the national health but it doesn't include the overtime.

Vera: But the cheque that's been made out does?

Kay: Yes.

Vera: You know why? Because that eleven pounds ten has been treated as – um – now what – what do you pay them? VAT. Yeah?

Kay: Oh, that's what it's been treated as, is it?

Vera: Yeah. Yeah. Not as part of the salary. So really that should be added back in. I tell you what to do. Can you alter your piece of paper to read what it should read and I'll alter mine. The cheque's right.

Kay: Yeah. Right. Okay, then.

Vera: Okay?

Kay: Yeah. Thanks, Vera. I think that's explained it. Thank you.

Vera: Yeah. Cheers.

Kay: Thanks.

Vera: Bye bye.

Kay: Ah. So it's been treated as VAT.

Joanna: This is a very friendly office. I think it helps having a lot of girls roughly the same age and as you can see they seem to have quite a lot of fun and laughs. But people do have the impression that office life can be very boring and it doesn't have to be like that.

UNIT TEN   The Exhibition

Announcer A: Good afternoon and welcome to the Daily Mail Ideal Home Exhibition. Catalogues are on sale at all entrances for only one pound forty. We hope you enjoy your visit to the exhibition today.

Interviewer: It really is an enormous exhibition, isn't it?

Organiser: Yes, indeed. It takes a long time to put together and we have about half a million square feet of floor space to fill every year. Er – we have around four hundred exhibitors each year and the number of people visiting – well – we expect the best part of a million is how we usually describe it. It'll be I suppose this year in the region of eight hundred thousand.

Announcer A: May we remind visitors to the show that there is a Child Playcare Centre sponsored by Volvo which is for children between the age of two and nine years old. This can be found on the ground floor to the right of the main entrance.

Announcer A: If you would like advice about money matters, visit Money Mail at the rear of the ground floor.

Interviewer: This gentleman here has about fifty tins of peas and a rather complicated-looking tin opener in his hand. What's so special about this tin opener? How does it work?

Salesman A: It's got a magnet on it. In actual fact, the magnet stops the lid going in the tin. And the cutting wheels cut right into the rim and it leaves the tin completely safe. You don't get any sharp edges on it. Now, unlike any other tin opener you can actually walk round the kitchen, go over to the sink and drain off at

any time. And when you do cut all the way round, you're not left with the magnet holding the lid and the dinner on the floor. The tin opener holds the tin, the magnet holds the lid. There are no sharp edges anywhere on that tin. I could take that right across my jugular and never ever cut myself.

Interviewer: This looks like a demonstration for some kind of furniture polish.

Salesman B: Come on – pay attention – we ask questions at the end. Right, shake the bottle up and what you do is – you pour a drop out into a bowl or a saucer. It doesn't matter how much you pour out because what you don't use goes back. You only need a damp cloth so don't just squeeze it out, wring it out. The more you wring out, the more there is as well to go back into that bottle to use again for another day.

Interviewer: What materials can you use it on then? All kinds of wood –

Salesman B: Any material. Paintwork – clean down your paintwork, all your furniture woods, any of these formicas in your kitchen. In other words, metals, absolutely everything except animal skins. Animal skins like hide and leather – they're like a sponge and they'll just suck it up.

Woman: You can use it on your kitchen wooden units, can you?

Salesman B: Yes.

Interviewer: You look quite impressed by this.

Woman: I am, yes. It looks as if it might work.

Interviewer: What's the most interesting thing you've seen today do you think?

Man: Well, we were just convinced by a demonstration upstairs on – er – miracle knives for home decorating and cutting tiles and the like. And we were convinced by the demonstration and bought the – bought the equipment.

Interviewer: Some of the salesmen are very good, aren't they?

Man: Yes, yes. I'm not actually – I'm not, I'm not easily taken in – I'm very – um – um – cautious – yeah, about people selling things like that but – um – it seemed cheap enough, so – er – for four pounds you've got four pieces of equipment – so we bought it.

Interviewer: What is it? – a special kind of knife?

Man: It's a knife for decorating and it's a sort of Stanley knife for cutting tiles and things like that and – er – a little knife, it's like, plastic, for cutting paper which is – you're not supposed to cut yourself with.

Announcer B: Would the parents of Mathew Brown, aged seven, from Upper Holloway, please come to the Information Desk which is on the ground floor at the Warwick Road entrance. Would the parents of Mathew Brown, aged seven, from Upper Holloway, please come to the Information Desk at the Warwick Road Entrance.

Interviewer: Well, I think this is the best place to be after a day at the exhibition – is lying flat on a water bed, as I've just done. Are they really full of water?

Salesman C: Yes, they are. Pure Earls Court water – all these beds are full of.

Interviewer: What happens if you stick a pin in it?

Salesman C: Well, then it would leak. It would cry like a little baby. It would come out like a tear drop. The water is not under pressure. It won't squirt out. And it's all contained within a safety liner inside the frame. So even if I took a knife and cut right across the mattress, the water could not get out of the bed.

Interviewer: Some people say that you should sleep on a very hard surface. I mean, these beds are very comfortable, but are they good for you?

Salesman C: Yes, they're extremely good. Er — chiropractors in Canada send people to our stores to buy water beds. They say, 'Go buy a water bed. It won't cure your back, but it will help.'

Interviewer: If you look round here at the people trying the beds out — they seem to think it's just a bit of a joke.

Salesman C: There is that problem. I don't know whether it's just the British. I think it maybe is. Last year in Norway — there's four point two million people live there – and they bought seventy-seven thousand water beds. In Canada, we have twenty-two percent of the population sleeping on water.

Interviewer: Right, well, I'm just going to lie down and have another few minutes before I go home.

Salesman C: Oh, you're most welcome.

UNIT ELEVEN   The News

Foreign Correspondent: . . . have already been destroyed. Police said that about five hundred homes were washed away by floods after Wayne struck the west coast of the island yesterday bringing driving rain and winds of up to eighty-four miles per hour. The typhoon flooded wide areas of Taiwan and crippled communications and power supplies. All domestic flights were cancelled yesterday and Taipei's Chiang Kai-shek international airport was closed for about five hours. Government radio reported that two passenger ferries had been sunk but gave no details of casualties. The work of emergency relief teams is being hampered by blocked roads and the loss of power and telephone communications in central regions. It will be some time before we hear the final casualty figures. This is Peter Donelly in Taipei.

Newsreader A: There will be another report from our correspondent in Taipei in the nine o' clock news tonight. And now here is a round-up of today's news:

Police in New York last night seized thirty-three kilos of pure heroin with a street value of seventy million dollars in what officials said was one of the biggest US drugs seizures in ten years.

The one month old occupation of a Michelin tyre factory in Belgium ended today when workers voted to accept an agreement which guarantees them full pay for a year.

The Soviet Union will help India prospect for on- shore oil under an agreement signed in Moscow today, the official news agency Tass reported.

And the main news today: Twenty-nine people were killed and ten were reported missing when Typhoon Wayne ripped across central Taiwan last night. And now over to Bob Taylor.

Newsreader B: Violence erupted in Ulster late last night after a loyalist parade in the mainly republican village of Rasharkin, County Antrim. Bottles and bricks were thrown as opposing factions clashed and eight RUC members and two civilians were injured, none of them seriously. Nine people were arrested. Police estimated that a hundred and fifty people had been involved in the violence during which the windows of two pubs and three houses were smashed.

Also in Northern Ireland, a part-time policeman has been injured in a terrorist attack in Ballymena, County Antrim. He was hit by shots fired from a car. His condition after an emergency operation is described as stable.

Seven men in Stoke were in custody today following a double stabbing which left one man dead and another injured. The pub fight was at the White Lion in North End Crescent and spread to a nearby fish and chip shop. Two motor bikes were set on fire during the incident. Police have appealed for witnesses to come forward.

And an eighty-three-year-old pensioner, Bill Williams, of Cheltenham, found himself in trouble with police over some innocent-looking plants. A passing drugs squad officer looked into his greenhouse and discovered that the plants were, in fact, cannabis. Mr Williams says, 'I've never used drugs in my life. I just thought the plants looked nice.' The police say there'll be no charges.

And now a travel flash from Jenny Browning:

Newsreader A: We have a message for drivers travelling south on the M6 in Lancashire. An accident on the southbound carriageway of the M6 in Lancashire is causing congestion and delays between junctions thirty-two and thirty-one near Preston. Drivers are asked to take extra care on the approach as the warning signals are out of action. The road should be clear in about an hour's time.

UNIT TWELVE   Sing Jazz

Shirin: Well, ever since I was child, you see, I've always wanted to be a singer and — er — it's just that I — er — I'm going — I want to start being a professional now. I'm going to start taking it seriously and that's why I'm here.

Donna: I wanted to learn about the jazz styles of singing — and that's why I came here.

Catherine: I've been singing for a number of years, many different styles, but, like Donna, I wanted also to find out about the jazz style.

Ken: Well, I've been a sort of frustrated jazz singer all my life, I suppose. I sing at home and all that and here's the first chance that I actually do it, learn a bit more about it and actually get to perform either in front of — or not in front of — people. Have a good time.

Paul: We're all here for the same reason.

Paul: It's flexibility, I think, and er . . . the opportunity to take a song which has been written maybe I don't know how many years ago and sung many times and make it your own because you can bring something individual to a song and jazz allows you that freedom of expression.

Catherine: Yeah, I mean the technical side is certainly a challenge and was a big challenge to me to learn the actual technique but it was also very good to actually put emotion into it. Jazz music is a great one to actually feel what you're doing and not think about it too much.

It's – it's – I mean – it's – you've got a lot of freedom – um – to do what you want and be creative but within certain confines.

Paul: Well, there are certain characteristics of instruments. I mean, for example, the saxophone, the trombone or the guitar and I think the jazz singer actually — or not all jazz singers — but — um — part of singing jazz is to take those characteristics of those instruments and incorporate them into the voice.

Shirin: I think my voice is quite powerful and and I think I've got quite a high emotional content — technically not so great.

Catherine: Yeah, I mean, I've learned that it's not so much — um — the voice but what you do with it — and also I also for a long time, and Shirin was the same, I always felt that it's the louder you sing the sort of better it is – and that one I've learned to change, I hope.

Ken: Yeah – well – I mean – I haven't got an incredibly good instrument in my voice and not all that marvellous a voice – you know

Others: rubbish

Ken: but – but – er – you say that to all the boys – but I think I've got a strong jazz feel.

Donna: It seems to me to be the most natural kind of music – er – certainly vocally and rhythmically – um – if anybody has a feel for music, jazz seems to be – er – the freeest type.

Shirin: Jazz is madness.

Donna: It's freedom.

Catherine: Freedom and fun.

Shirin: Well – I want to make it for Carnegie Hall and – um – all them places – seriously.

Donna: Seriously I want to be the best, I do – I do.

Karen: I haven't got any set plans because I mean if I did that I think I'd be terribly disappointed if they all collapsed. Just – just to sing and perhaps – earn a sort of reasonable decent living from it.

Ken: I don't have ambitions in any sort of professional sense just want to – because I enjoy doing it so much – I just want to be as good as I can at it and that's all.

Paul: Well, I want to make a career out of it and want to be singing all the time and not have to bother with any other kinds of activity – and – well – to reach as high as I can.

UNIT THIRTEEN   On the Agenda

Carol: . . . . I think we've covered everything there so I'd like to ask the meeting if they agree that these minutes are –

Steve: Hi, everybody. Sorry. Sorry I'm late.

Brian/Carol: Hullo, Steve.

Steve: . . . the longest lecture I've ever been to in my life.

Carol: We've just done the minutes but I'm asking the meeting if we all agree that these are a correct record of the meeting of May twentieth.

Brian/Meg: Yes. Seconded.

Carol: Right. We'll move on now to item three, Matters arising.

Steve: Oh. Look, have you got an agenda? I've forgotten my agenda.

Carol: Oh, yes. There you are.

Steve: Oh, thanks.

Carol: Brian, would you make any note of anything that comes up in this section.

Brian: Yes, certainly, Madame Chair.

Meg: Well, I'm afraid I've got a complaint to make about this. Um – I – as you know, I missed the meeting before last because I had flu. And I couldn't believe that the date of the last meeting was fixed for May the twentieth. I mean it's just – it's such a crazy time to choose. We were all revising. I couldn't get to it because I'd got an exam the next day and no way I was going to jeopardise that. So, basically, I'd just like to say can we make sure that when we – when we – when we do fix these dates that we actually do take account of what's – of what everyone's timetable is and just – um – put me – put me complaint on record.

Carol: Fair enough. OK. Anybody else anything to say?

Steve: Well – yes – er – no – I think that's very reasonable. Just it must be a bit difficult sometimes to – er – fix it with everybody's timetable.

Brian: That's right.

Meg: Yeah, but exam time is just crazy. You got to – you got to leave it till after exams or – or – give people plenty of time.

Brian: It's a question of losing one monthly meeting.

Carol: We have to plan ahead, you see. This is the thing. It has to be timed with the following term and it's a question of fitting in with as many people as we can.

Meg: Yeah, I know. But exams happen with everybody.

Brian: I think we can't really afford to lose a meeting.

Carol: No, this is the problem.

Meg: No, no. I'm not saying lose a meeting, but saying make sure that it's not in the middle of exam time, you know.

Brian: Reasonable.

Carol: Yes. Fair enough. OK. Now on to item four, next year's programme. Now we've settled on the six films to be shown next term but unfortunately – um – it's not possible to show the Japanese film that we'd all chosen. But we've got two possible alternatives to this – have come up.

Meg: What were those?

Carol: One is Polanski's *Knife in the Water*. Possibly his first film, made around the fifties. And the other one is *Butch Cassidy and the Sundance Kid* with Paul Newman and Robert Redford. Now any opinions about this?

Brian: Well – er – Madame Chair

Carol: Before we go to vote.

Brian: Yes – um – well – I mean – I think – er – for me, there's – there's no choice. I mean I think we must go for the Polanski.

Meg: Absolutely. I agree.

Brian: Er – you know – *Butch Cassidy and the Sundance Kid* is a very good example of a – you know – a genre picture.

Steve: Oh, it's a great film. It's a good laugh.

Brian: But – well –

Meg: You can get that from a video library.

Brian: Absolutely.

Steve: Yeah. But we get . . . . so many foreign films. This next season is full of foreign, serious, heavy films. Couldn't we have a nice, light, jokey one?

Brian: I would disagree with you there, Steve. I – I mean – I don't think we get enough – er –

Steve: Look. It's a good, well-made film – *Butch Cassidy and the Sundance Kid* – which is a good example of film technique. Let's not be snobby about this.

Meg: It's not being snobby at all.

Carol: I think we'd better put this to the vote. Fair enough. Everybody will have a say. Now who's for *Butch Cassidy and the Sundance Kid*?

Steve: Yeah. I am, yeah. I like American films.

Carol: And *Knife in the Water*? Right. *Knife in the Water* it is. Sorry about that, Steve.

Everyone: Right. Right.

Carol: Item five. Elections. I'd like to remind everyone and would you be so kind as to remind other members who aren't present – that nominations for Chair, Secretary and Treasurer for next year should be made by the end of next week. That is, before the AGM.

Brian: Ah. Point of order, Madam Chairman – um – person. Madam Chair. Er – the club's rules do allow people to make nominations at the AGM. Er – so – er – the urgency isn't there.

Carol: Right. Point taken, Brian. Thank you.

Steve: Yeah, but it's easier if they're in before, isn't it?

Brian: Well, obviously, yes. But you can make nominations at the AGM.

Carol: Right. Item six – Financial matters.

Meg: Oh, hang on. I just wanted – just – er – before you go on to item six. I just want to propose a vote of thanks to Carol for all her work as Chair during the past year. I mean – we're very grateful. It's a rotten job. You've got to get us all together and – er – thanks very much for doing it.

Brian: Seconded.

Carol: Thank you.

Brian: Well done, Carol.

Steve: Yeah and while we're on that, I'd like to propose a vote of thanks to Brian for – for – er – being a Secretary.

Carol: Yes, indeed.

Steve: That's a lot of work getting all the notices out for the meetings and things – it's – er – even if we do disagree about foreign films.

Brian: I'll treat you to *Butch Cassidy* when it's showing down the local.

Carol: And on to item six, Financial Matters. We can't deal with that tonight because John's away. So he'll give the Treasurer's report at the AGM.

Everyone: Right.

Carol: And, finally, item seven. We've got to agree on a date for the next Committee meeting. It should be sometime around the second week in October.

Meg: I was – I was going to suggest – why don't we do it on the tenth, the Tuesday, because we've got the union meeting that day. So we could – if we fix the meeting for six o'clock just before the union meeting, we might be able to get some more members.

Carol: Yes. That's a good idea.

Meg: Everybody's going to be there anyway.

Everyone: Yeah. Right.

Carol: What does everybody else feel about that? That's the tenth. Does that sound all right?

Steve: Sounds very reasonable. Yeah.

Brian: Er –

Carol: Brian?

Brian: – er – yes –

Steve: That's Tuesday – is it Tuesday the tenth?

Meg: Yeah – The union meeting is about – I think – it's eight o'clock. So if we do it at six.

Carol: Six o'clock on Tuesday the tenth of October.

Brian: That should give us plenty of time.

Steve: Yeah. Good idea.

Carol: That's terrific. Thank you very much everybody. I'll call the meeting to a conclusion.

Everyone: Right. Great.

Steve: Ah – I'm off to the union for a drink. Who's coming?

Brian: Right. I'll drink to that. I'll buy you some Polish vodka, Steve.

UNIT FOURTEEN   The Maniac Mile

Announcer: Reporter Chris Hawksworth went along to talk to the organiser and meet some of the participants before the race started.

Chris: Just tell me how the event originated – how it began and the organisation of it, will you?

Organiser: Well – er – this is an extension of my uphill race in as much as I started with what I call 'the murder mile'. It's a mile uphill and I've just reversed it and this is the downhill and this is 'the maniac'.

Chris: And what about the gradient? Because even walking I'm getting puffed walking up this.

Organiser: It's one in ten approximately.

Chris: One in ten.

Organiser: One in ten.

Chris: What is the aim of it? To give everybody a run and to- or to break records or to what?

Organiser: Er – a bit of both. Obviously, the people who enjoy the event – they enjoy the social gathering afterwards. Er – but to the more serious athletes obviously it's the – it's dipping below four minutes.

Chris: Are you going to break four minutes?

Runner 1: No. Hardly.

Runner 2: Yeah. Three fifty-nine last year.

Chris: I bet you'll be glad when you're running down, won't you?

Runner 3: I'll be jolly glad when it's over. Last time I ran this race it nearly destroyed me.

Chris: Did it?

Runner 3: It's like – er – it's like – er er – it's sadism, you know.

Chris: Do you think you'll break four minutes tonight?

Runner 3: Yeah. I did three fifty-four last time.

Chris: Good luck, anyway.

Chris: Are you going to break four minutes tonight?

Runner 4: No, I don't think so.

Chris: What are you hoping for?

Runner: 4 No idea. Haven't a clue.

Chris: You haven't done it before?

Runner 4: No. Never done it.

Chris: Could you be the first woman to break four minutes tonight?

Runner 5: Not a chance. Not a chance.

Chris: What are you hoping for?

Runner 5: I'll just be very happy to get down. In about ten minutes.

Chris: I see you've got a good seat there.

Spectator 1: Of course. Yes.

Chris: I suppose by the time they get down to here they're going really fast, aren't they? Did you –?

Spectator 2: I should imagine so.

Chris: Have you seen it before? Do you always watch it?

Spectator 2: Well, I prefer it the other way up. Coming uphill not going down. It's too easy going down.

Chris: That's because you're a masochist, I think.

Spectator 2: I think I am, yes. Well, it makes it more exciting.

Chris: Why aren't you taking part in it this year?

Spectator 2: er . . .

Chris: I mean it's downhill all the way.

Spectator 2: If there's somebody standing by with a stretcher, I will.

Spectator 3: She's just had a perm.

Spectator 2: Now there you are.

Spectator 3: She's just had her hair done.

Spectator 2: I've just had me hair done and I don't want to spoil it.

Spectator 1: She's frightened of falling, aren't you . . .?

Chris: And here come the first bunch and they're about two hundred yards from the finishing line. It seems to be harder running downhill. Here come some more. It's a fine night. Come on. You can do it.

Runner: Thanks.

Chris: And this is the only event I know where the band plays continuously even when the race is taking place. In fact, when people come past the finishing line, the band is still playing on regardless as the first person to break four minutes breaks the tape.

Chris: How was it?

Runner 6: Oh, terrible. It really was.

Chris: How'd you do?

Runner 7: Oh, it's hard. Oh.

Chris: What speed did you do? What did you do? What time?

Runner 7: Five ten.

Chris: Are you happy with that?

Runner 7: Very.

Chris: I'm talking to the winner.

Winner: Hullo.

Chris: What did you do? What speed?

Winner: I think it was about three thirty two.

Chris: So that's five seconds still outside the record?

Winner: That is. Yeah.

Chris: Yeah. Do conditions in a mile like this matter a lot? I mean I suppose when you're running downhill as opposed to the flat?

Winner: If it'd been a torrential downpour, it would've been tougher. But the conditions tonight were okay. They were perfect, I thought.

Chris: How was it?

Runner 3: It was bloody hard, but I did it.

Chris: What did you do?

Runner 3: Three fifty-one forty-seven.

Chris: Ah, so you — so what you came for you've achieved?

Runner 3: Absolutely. Yeah.

Chris: What about yourself?

Runner 8: Er — the same as last year. Nice and fast.

Chris: How much different is it from running on the flat though? Presumably it shakes you up a lot more?

Runner 8: I don't — it's impossible to compare it to a — to what I might call a normal race. It's — like it is — it's the maniac mile.

Chris: What different technique of running do you have to have?

Runner 8: You have to loosen the bolts on your head before you do it. All right?

UNIT FIFTEEN Acid Rain

Adam: I'm going to talk about acid rain, a subject which many people have heard of but very few understand fully. I'm going to talk about exactly what acid rain is and why it's a problem and then I'm going to finish off by saying what we can do about it, what the solutions are now and what the solutions will be in the future, in the long term. So first of all, acid rain is a term that's really being used now for a kind of pollution which is hanging over our heads in a sense — it's the air pollution above us. It's the pollution that's coming down in rain, in mist, in snow, in hail, in many different ways and damaging our forests, our lakes and rivers, our buildings and even human health. If we are to control acid rain, we must know what is actually causing it, so now I'm going to talk about the chemicals involved. There are really three we should look at. These are sulphur dioxide, nitrogen oxides and ozone. The first two of those are primary pollutants — that is they are produced directly from source. In the case of sulphur dioxide, the main problem is power station chimneys. In the case of nitrogen oxides, they come really half and half from cars and from power stations. Ozone is what's known as a secondary pollutant. It means it's formed in the atmosphere from a combination of other pollutants, other primary pollutants. Ozone is formed from a combination of nitrogen oxides and hydrocarbons both of which come from car exhausts. If you put sunlight onto these two chemicals, they react together and they form ozone and so the highest levels of ozone are found in a hot summer around the edges of cities where there

are lots of car exhausts, lots of sunlight and then you end up with a lot of ozone.

I think the one that most people would associate with acid rain, if they know anything about it at all, is sulphur and particularly sulphur dioxide.

About seventy-one percent of all the sulphur dioxide emitted from Britain comes from the large coal burning power stations predominantly situated in the Midlands. In fact, Britain is Western Europe's largest emitter of sulphur dioxide. We put out some three point seven million tons a year. That's more than any other country except perhaps Poland or Russia if you go to the East block. The problem, of course, with sulphur dioxide is that it doesn't just fall close to the factory or the power station. It gets lifted into the air and it can travel thousands of miles in the air before it falls as rain. So we're not just creating a problem for ourselves, we're creating a problem for the rest of Europe. And that is really why the Scandinavians and the Dutch and the Belgians have become angry with the British government because it hasn't done anything about acid rain — because they are paying for the environmental damage which is caused by our pollution. But we shouldn't think that all our pollution goes out of the country. Our environment is dying as well and sulphur from our power stations is landing all over the United Kingdom. In Wales and in the West of Scotland, acid rain is already having quite a marked effect. Some hundreds of lakes in Wales have been affected, several have lost their fish and in the West of Scotland, twenty-seven Galloway lakes have already completely lost their fish.

Now perhaps I should go on to some of the solutions that we should be looking to to stop this environmental catastrophe. There are short-term solutions and there are long-term solutions. In the short term, we need to make immediate cuts to the emissions that are coming from our power stations and cars. In the long term, we need to change the way society is thinking. Many people have heard of the thirty percent club. This is a group of now some twenty-two nations which have agreed to cut their sulphur emissions by thirty percent on nineteen eighty levels by the year nineteen ninety-three. Britain hasn't yet joined the thirty percent club. Some of the other countries that have are Sweden, Norway, Canada, West Germany, the Netherlands — even Russia has joined the thirty percent club. This is only the first step on the road to effective sulphur emission control. And what we really want to see is reductions of between sixty and ninety percent over the next ten years or so. And looking to the longer term, we shouldn't just rely on solutions that involve a technological fix. We shouldn't just clean up power station chimneys and car exhausts. What we need to do is change the way society thinks and reacts. The first thing that needs to be done is we need to use less energy. One way of using less energy is to increase recycling and so recycling schemes and re-use of materials should be encouraged throughout Europe and North America. Secondly, we have to change our transport system. We have to look for a more efficient transport system which relies less on individuals' use of cars and more on a good public transport — er — network. These are the things we must be looking forward to. Unless we do that, unless we change society in this way — conserve energy, rationalise our way of transport and now clean up our power stations and individual cars — then we're bound to see more and worse environmental effects from air pollution and acid rain. We must act now.

ANSWER KEY

UNIT ONE An American in London

Extensive listening

1 a) ii) He is interested in getting to know Britain. Although Mathew notices some differences between Britain and America, he is not negative about these. He is interested in the way young people in London think and behave. The only thing he says he does not like is the way young women often wear black. He is quite positive about everything else. He is trying to adapt to the driving ('you have to teach yourself to look the other way') and the language differences ('I'm starting to pick it up now') which he enjoys ('they're funny'). He does not sound unhappy about anything.
   The words that describe Mathew are:
   b) 1 *polite* – He does not want to sound rude when asked if he dislikes young women's clothes. He says 'Not really. That's just my preference.'
   2 *frank* – He is open about his opinions ('I'd rather see different colours.') but not intolerant, for example, about men wearing earrings.
   3 *cheerful* – He sounds amused by the differences he has noticed such as driving on the other side of the road and the language differences. He does not seem depressed by anything.
   4 *thoughtful* – When asked about young people's political awareness and knowledge of other countries, Mathew thinks carefully about his answers ('Um – that's a good question – um – well, I think that . . .')
   5 *friendly* – He enjoys talking to someone about his experiences and giving his opinions.
   6 *relaxed* – He seems relaxed all through the interview; not shy or nervous.

Intensive listening

1 a)

British English	American English
queue	*line*
chips	*French fries*
crisps	potato chips

   b) *mate* and *love*.

> Mathew has heard these words used frequently in London in shops and on buses or trains. 'Mate' is used in London between friends and in a friendly way to strangers. It is most often said to men. 'Love' is used in many parts of Britain between friends and in a friendly way to women and children generally. It is usually only said to a man by other members of the family or intimate friends.

2 Picture c.

3

	Britain	USA
young people	● more [1]*radical* in politics	● not as much
young people's knowledge of other countries	● more politically [2]*aware* ● know all about the US and how it's [3]*run*	● just have a [4]*vague* understanding of a few other countries
reasons (mainly because of the[5] *press*)	● hear a lot about America ● US policies [6]*affect* Britain	● don't hear as much about [7]*Britain* ● Britain's policies [8]*don't* affect USA as much

Study point

1 a) I've never seen so many men wearing earrings before.
      or I never saw so many men wearing earrings before.
   b) There are a few differences in the language.
      or I (do) notice a few differences in the language.
   c) Young people's clothes in America are much more colourful than those in London.
   d) There is a lot about the United States in the British press whereas in American newspapers you don't see that much about Britain.
   e) Young people in the United States are not as politically aware as young people in Britain.

2 Possible answers:
   a) Well, I'd say the British people are more reserved than Americans.
   b) I think they seem to be more politically aware than their parents' generation.
   c) I think the reason is that education has improved generally.
   d) I like wearing jeans and T-shirts best. That's just my own preference.
   e) I'd rather visit America.

UNIT TWO Visiting India

Extensive listening

1 They talked about *food, the weather, sightseeing* and *things to buy*.

2 a) *false* – They went at different times of the year. Marsha went in June–July and Julia went over the Christmas period.
   b) *true* – They both went to Srinagar, in Kashmir.
   c) *false* – Marsha says she never had a hot curry and describes the food as mild. Julia agrees the food was edible. She means it was not too hot for her to eat.
   d) *true* – They both say the food was wonderful and sound very enthusiastic. Julia thinks the vegetables are beautiful and Marsha loves the pureed spinach.

e) *true* – From the way Julia and Marsha say together 'Oh, the gardens. Yes.' we can tell they both enjoyed visiting them very much.
f) *false* – They suggest that 'everything' in Kashmir is a bargain and that they were tempted to bring back many things. They mention silk, honey, wood carvings and things made of papier maché as well as the bedspread Marsha bought and the rug which Julia bought.

Intensive listening

1 a) (ii) Srinagar is in the hills.
b) (ii) Srinagar is cooler than Delhi.
c) (i) Marsha had pumpkin in yoghurt sauce.
d) (i) They grow many vegetables in Kashmir.

2 a) (ii) filled
b) (i) sheltering
c) (ii) bottom
d) (i) wonderful

3

a) Marsha's bedspread	b) wood carvings	c) papier maché
i) cotton	i) e.g. cigarette boxes	i) e.g. *boxes*
ii) *quilted*	ii) e.g. *bowls*	ii) e.g. *trays*
iii) handwork	iii) made of *maple*	iii) e.g. *cocktail mats*
	iv) inlaid *mother-of-pearl*	iv) painted with *gold leaf*

Study point

f) incomplete   e) rephrasing
1 Liz: What about – didn't you say something about – before – about some gardens?
Marsha: Oh, the gardens. Yes. } a) speaking at same
Julia: Yes.   } time
Marsha: There are dozens of Mogul gardens. We –
b) interruption
Liz: What are the Moguls?
Julia: Shalimar. Oh, Mogul.
Marsha: Mogul. That was from the Mogul period.
c) hesitation
That was – what – eighteenth century?
Julia: Yes.
Marsha: The Mogul emperors built these gardens
b) interruption
and they have a –
Julia: Very formal.
Marsha: Yes. There's a pattern to all of them. With –
c) hesitation
there's a – they're on several levels – terraces.
e) rephrasing
They're terraced.
Julia: Yes.

> Listening to an informal conversation on tape is sometimes difficult because of these features. But if you are taking part in the conversation or watching it, these features do not cause so much difficulty because you can see the expression on people's faces and their gestures or other movements.

2 a) Would you recommend the northern part?
b) Whereabouts would you suggest I go?
c) When do you think is the best time to go?
d) How would you advise me to spend my time?

e) What things are absolutely unmissable?
f) Is the museum worth a visit?
g) What sort of bargains should I look for?
h) Are the wood carvings worth buying?

UNIT THREE   Before Breakfast

Extensive listening

1 a) *true* – They met in Cornwall.
b) *true* – Joanna was only twelve years old but she fell in love with Tom.
c) *false*
d) *true*
e) *false* – She says he is 'unkind' and she wants to go and sit at another table. (But then she decides to stay so perhaps she does like him underneath. What do you think?)
f) *true* – He doesn't want her to go away. He persuades her to stay.

Intensive listening

1 a) They both like to eat a big breakfast.
b) They both like coffee.
c) They both have their coffee white.

2 **Joanna:** But we were in love.
Tom: I've never been in love.
Joanna: Then you were lying to me. You declared your undying passion.
Tom: Look. This is getting embarrassing. The next thing you're going to tell me is that we're married.

3 a) You can if you can bend your knees.
Tom is playing on the two meanings of can: (i) meaning permission e.g Can I smoke? and (ii) meaning ability e.g. Can you swim?
b) Yes, I do. (Honestly?) Yes. You're the girl who came and sat down at this table a couple of minutes ago.
Tom is pretending not to understand Joanna.
c) Now you come to mention it – (Yes?) And now that I look at you more closely – (Yes?) I don't believe I've ever seen you before in my life.
Tom is teasing Joanna. He leads her to think that he may remember her, but then says that he doesn't.
d) You've ordered breakfast.
Tom is sorry that he has upset Joanna and hurt her feelings. But instead of saying that this is the real reason he wants her to stay, he pretends it is because she has ordered breakfast.

Study point

1 a) I'm not aware that you do know my name.
b) Well, I have to admit that you do know my name. My first name, anyway.
c) (Then) it's all a case of mistaken identity.
d) (But) I have absolutely no recollection of you.
e) I've got a feeling that if we start off as if we've only just met, things might turn out differently.
f) I think we might get to like each other quite a bit.

2 a) (i) You might as well enjoy it.
b) (ii) Don't you remember my name?
c) (ii) We started off badly.

UNIT FOUR Looking Back

Extensive listening

1 These topics are mentioned:
*birthdays a river a grandmother
a wedding schooldays a pet
the countryside*

2
a) *there* refers to the river Thames, particularly the little 'beach' where John and his family used to go.
b) *That* refers to the time when Barbara was a bridesmaid and went to the wedding in a big limousine.
c) *It* refers to the bullying at John's school.
d) *The poor old dear* refers to John's grandmother.
e) *it* refers to stepping on the budgie and killing it.

Intensive listening

1
a) 5
b) pink with flowers

2
a) (ii) a child with no brothers or sisters
b) (i) far from other towns or villages
c) (i) of poor appearance

3
a) *true* – He says he was very frightened of the dark.
b) *false* – He doesn't say anything about spiders or other insects.
c) *true* – She says 'I just had nightmares.'
d) *true* – She says 'I was frightened to close me eyes in case I'd die.'
e) *false* – John says there was a lot of bullying at the school.
f) *true* – John says 'it was carting young lads off behind the bicycle sheds and thumping them.'

4
a) *John* – to his grandmother after he jumped off the window sill
b) *Peter's father* – to his family after he trod on the budgie
c) *John's grandmother* – to John after he jumped off the window sill
d) *Peter* – to his father when the budgie died in his hands
e) *John's mother* – to John after he jumped off the window sill

Study point

1
a) 1 lived or used to live (habitual state)
   2 used to take (habitual action)
   3 used to have or had (habitual state)
   4 happened (completed action)
   5 used to let (habitual action)
   6 put (completed action)
   7 trod (completed action)
   8 were (temporary state)
b) would take, would let (habitual actions)

2
a) This great big limousine came for
   { me and my brother.
   { my brother and I. (more formal)
   We were sitting in the back and I was waving like the Queen.
b) We was always round someone's house.
   It was all good fun when we was kids.
   I was frightened to close me eyes in case I'd die.

Students who have studied English for several years in their own countries may still find it difficult to understand people in Britain when they first arrive. There could be several reasons for this: people may speak much faster than students are used to, they may use a lot of colloquial and idiomatic language or they may have a regional accent or dialect and use non-standard forms like Barbara does. Students will get used to all of these things in time although a very strong accent or special regional dialect may still give problems. Don't worry too much about this; sometimes even British people from different parts of the country cannot understand each other very well! There are many different accents in *Soundtracks* but none of them are very difficult to understand.

UNIT FIVE The Long Essay

Extensive listening

An undergraduate is someone who is studying for a first degree: a BA or a BSc. A postgraduate student is someone who already has a first degree and is now studying for a postgraduate diploma of some kind which may be a professional qualification, an MA or an MSc.

1
a) She is a teacher.
b) She comes from Malaysia.

2
a) iii) changed considerably
   Her original title was rather vague. The new title is much more specific.
b) i) everything she had in her first draft
   It will be relevant to 7–11 year-old children in London and in Malaysia. The materials will include stories and poems.
c) ii) both Selvi and the tutor are pleased
   Selvi says the new plan is 'Very, very impressive. Very good.' The tutor says it 'sounds very, very interesting'.

Intensive listening

1
b) She is going to write some poems herself.

2
TITLE Using a topic-based approach to the teaching of *English as a second language to 7–11 year-old bilingual children*
DESCRIPTION
PART 1 Context
   a) *London*
   b) Malaysia
PART 2 *Criteria*
   a) *motivation*
   b) *multi-cultural*
   c) communicative
   d) *cross-curricular*
   e) *integrated skills*
PART 3 *Materials' Topic*
PART 4 *Comments*

   • poems
   • *stories*
   • *tasks*

Study point

1 a) I think what we need (actually) is a slightly more specific plan.
  b) Shall we see if we can make a plan?
  c) Let's (just) list the things we've mentioned.
  d) Can we go through them?
  e) Does that make sense to you – if we put it like that?

2 a) multi-cultural
  b) bilingual
  c) cross-curricular
  d) misunderstood
  e) sub-sections
  f) rearranged

3

	Singular	Plural
Nouns from Greek	*criterion* phenomenon *hypothesis* crisis	criteria *phenomena* hypotheses *crises*
Nouns from Latin	medium *curriculum* bacterium	*media* curricula *bacteria*

UNIT SIX   A Sense of Humour

Extensive listening

1 c)

2 a) *false* – Sandy thinks there are different senses of humour in different parts of Britain. He says Britain or Great Britain when, in fact, he is talking about the United Kingdom (Great Britain and Northern Ireland) as well as Eire (the Republic of Ireland).
  b) *false* – He thinks that's one of the difficulties with humour in Great Britain.
  c) *true* – The last story he tells is an example of this.
  d) *false* – Sandy thinks you do need to know something about the language and culture of a people in order to understand their humour.
  e) *true* – He says they are 'quintessentially Irish' and 'typically Irish'.

Intensive listening

1 a) What's time to pigs?
  b) The winter's lovely. They die like flies.

2 1 regional   3 strike   5 plays
  2 problems   4 strike   6 usages

3 a) I'm no going.
  b) He's no coming today.
  c) Will ye no come back again?
     (This is a line from a well-known Scottish folk song.)
  d) Do you no know No No Nanette?

4 At the end, Sandy says 'things are funny or not' and the friend says 'Or no.' He is using 'no' for 'not' again, in the Scottish way.

Study point

1 a) i) I know a true story which/that epitomises the Irish sense of humour.
     ii) It was a friend of mine who was working in the south of Ireland.
     iii) There are regional senses of humour which/that are all very different.
     iv) It is a musical comedy which/that was written in the twenties.
     v) A person was singing with an opera company which/that was on tour in Edinburgh.
     vi) He went into a flower shop to buy some flowers for a friend who was going on to do the performance that night.

  b) i) I know a true story epitomising the Irish sense of humour.
     ii) It was a friend of mine working in the south of Ireland.
     iii) There are regional senses of humour and they are all very different.
     There are regional senses of humour, all of them very different.
     iv) It is a musical comedy written in the twenties.
     v) A person was singing with an opera company on tour in Edinburgh.
     vi) He went in a flower shop to buy some flowers for a friend going on to do the performance that night.

     Notice the use of the present participle in i), ii) and vi) and the past participle in iv).

2 **Lady:** Excuse me. Are you in show business?
  Singer: Yes, I am, actually.
  Lady: I thought so. You can always tell.
  Singer: Really?
  Lady: Oh, yes. I used to be in show business myself.
  Singer: Really?
  Lady: I was in 'No No Nannette'.
       Do you no know 'No No Nannette'?

UNIT SEVEN   A Card Trick

Teacher's note
You may wish to change your classroom procedure for this Unit in the following way.
For a class of twenty students, you will need five packs of cards. Go through the *Pre-listening* work with the whole class. Then divide the class into four groups. Give each group a pack of cards. One student from each group goes into a corner of the room to listen to the tape together without the rest of the class hearing. They should take a pack of cards with them. Meanwhile, students in the other groups can use their cards to test each other on the vocabulary or to show each other any card games they know. When the students listening to the tape are sure that they understand how to do the trick, they go back to their groups and try out the trick. If someone in the group knows how the trick is done, he or she can do it with another student. The students who know how the trick is done should not tell the others. When everyone has seen the trick done successfully, play the tape to the whole class and work through the *Extensive and Intensive listening* exercises as usual.

Extensive listening

1 b) and c)

Intensive listening

1 1 – c), 2 – g), 3 – a), 4 – d), 5 – f), 6 – e), 7 – b).

2 a) before
   b) a good way
   c) at the end
   d) below

Follow-up

1 a) This is how you can make the triangle point
      downwards by moving only three coins.

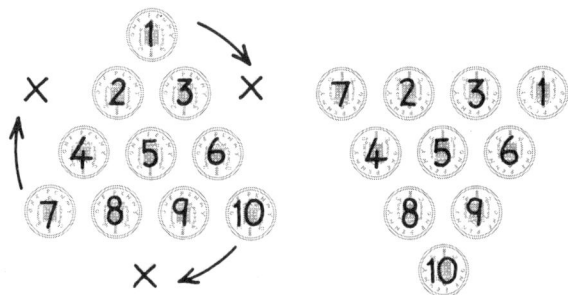

   Move coin 1 next to coin 3.
   Move coin 10 below and between coins 8 and 9.
   Move coin 7 next to coin 2.

   b) Here is an example of the way this trick works.
      Your friend opens the book at page 20.
      She chooses line 3 and then she chooses word 2 on
      line 3.

Double the number of the page.	40
Multiply by 5 and add 20.	220
Add the number of the line plus 5.	228
Multiply by ten.	2280
Add the number of the word in the line.	2282
Subtract 250 from the total.	2032

   The first two numbers tell you the page. It is page
   20.
   The next number tells you the line. It is line 3.
   The last one is the word number. It is the second
   word.

Study point

1 a) need
   b) Please . . . . . . have to
   c) Don't
   d) must . . . . If . . . . . can't
   e) A good way to do it is
   f) This is the moment
   g) got to

2 a) *it* refers to the card I (the magician) saw
   b) *it* refers to your (the other person's) card
   c) *it* refers to the bottom card of the pack
   d) *it* refers to looking at the bottom card of the pack
   e) *that* refers to looking at the bottom card of the
      pack
   f) *it* refers to the bottom card of the pack

UNIT EIGHT   The Macbeth Ordeal

Teacher's note
You may wish to change your classroom procedure
for this Unit by stopping the tape at certain points and
asking the students to predict what happens next. You
can do this at four points, as follows: 1) After Emma says
'Ha, ha. Most hilarious' and leaves slamming the door.
2) When Gerry has arrived at Alison's and after he says
'I was to sleep in the attic'. 3) When Gerry arrives at
the Hibernian hotel and after he says 'so I rang the
bell'. 4) At the end of the story.
Do not spend too long at each point or students may lose
interest in the story. Also, do not spend too long at the
end of the story asking students what they think
happened next because they are given time to do this in
the *Follow-up*, exercise 2.

Extensive listening

1 b) He did not decide to break up with his girlfriend
      although this did happen. He did not predict he
      would have a lot of problems. In fact, Gerry was
      optimistic throughout the story. He was always
      hoping for the best.

2 1 c), 2 e), 3 a), 4 b), 5 f), 6 d).

3 a) He was *eager* when he was offered the title role in
      Macbeth. He wanted to accept.
   b) He was *stubborn* when his girlfriend told him not
      to grow a beard. He refused to change his mind.
   c) He was *apologetic* when he arrived at Alison's
      cottage. He was sorry to disturb her so late at
      night.
   d) He felt *ill* when he woke up with an asthma attack.
   e) He was *cold* when he was walking around looking
      for a hotel in the middle of the night.
   f) He was *relieved* when the manager told him there
      was a vacancy at the hotel. He was pleased that his
      search to find somewhere to sleep had finally
      ended.
   g) He was *shocked* when the manager's wife
      screamed and said that he had taken a thousand
      pounds.
   h) He was *resigned* when he realised he would not
      get any sleep that night. He knew he would have to
      answer the policeman's questions.

Intensive listening

1 He himself refers to *Macbeth* as 'the Scottish play'.
   Also, when he saw the cats he crossed his fingers for
   luck.

2 a) i)   You must take responsibility for this action.
   b) iii) a day when everything goes wrong
   c) ii) I don't like them very much.

Study point

1 a) Nevertheless . . . despite   e) and
   b) however   f) Although
   c) but   g) As
   d) so

2 a) had . . . . had spent
   b) arrived . . . . . had been travelling
   c) woke . . . . . had probably been playing
   d) turned . . . . saw . . . . . assumed

Extensive listening

1 a) i) The conversation Cathy has with Julie asking for a code number and the conversation between Vera and Kay about a problem with an invoice are both inter-departmental calls. In the case of the first call made by Anne Biggs we do not know. It might be an outside call or an inter-departmental call.
ii) There is one outside call which a secretary takes for her boss. We do not know if this is a personal call or a business call.

   b) i) In the first call, Anne Biggs leaves a message for Geoff Corbet. In the third call, the secretary is about to take a message when her boss comes to the phone and speaks to the person himself.
iii) In the second call, Cathy is asking for information. She wants to know an account code number.
v) In the last call, Vera and Kay are dealing with a problem concerning an invoice.

2 a) *agree* – She says you need patience 'particularly if you're dealing with the public'.
   b) *disagree* – She says if you work as a private secretary you have to be 'almost a buffer between the public and your boss'. This means you sometimes have to judge whether your boss really wants to talk to the person then or not.
   c) *disagree* – She says the atmosphere is 'very friendly' and the girls have 'a lot of fun and laughs', but she does not say that she thinks this is a bad thing. She sounds as if she thinks it is a good thing.
   d) *agree* – She says having a lot of girls the same age helps make a friendly atmosphere and that office life 'doesn't have to be boring'.

Intensive listening

1 a) To: Geoff Corbett
      From: *Anne Biggs*
          Please phone her on extension *3136*. She wants to book some *orders* in and she has a *quote*.
   b) To:
      From: Cathy
          The account number you wanted is 4 *W09 74600500*.

2 1 routine   3 freelance
   2 invoices   4 sort

3 a) i) The salary cheque was correct.
      Kay says 'the actual cheque was made out for the right amount' and later Vera confirms 'the cheque's right'.
   b) ii) The invoice is incorrect.
      The figures are wrong. Kay says 'there seems to be a differing figure' and at the end Vera says she should alter her piece of paper, i.e. the invoice.
   c) i) Both Vera and Kay change the invoice.
      Vera says 'Can you alter your piece of paper to read what it should read and I'll alter mine.'

Study point

1 a) There is sometimes more than one way to complete the conversation. Some alternatives are given here.

Caller:	Can/Could you give me extension 3044, please?
	Can/Could you put me through to extension 3044, please?
Secretary:	Hullo. Accounts.
Caller:	May/Can/Could I speak to John Mellor, please?
Secretary:	Just a moment./Hold on a moment. Hullo. I'm afraid he's not in his office at the moment.
Caller:	Do you know when he's likely to be back?
	Can/Could you tell me when he's likely to be back?
Secretary:	In about an hour. Can/May I take a message?/ Would you like to leave a message?/ Would you like me to give him a message?
Caller:	Just tell him Mary Slade phoned and ask him to ring me back.
Secretary:	Does he have your number?
Caller:	No, it's 948
Secretary:	948
Caller:	3266
Secretary:	3266. All right. I'll see that he gets the message.
Caller:	Thank you. Goodbye.

   b) None of these sentences are very formal.
   These are the more informal sentences in each pair.
   i)   Is he around today?
   ii) Just a moment.
   iii) Can you hang on a second?
   iv) Sorry. I've no idea where he is.
   v)   It's Mary Slade here.
   You would use the more informal sentences when speaking to a friend or colleague.
   You would probably use the less informal sentences when speaking to your boss. But this depends on your boss. If your boss is friendly and informal with his staff, you might use the more informal language.
   You would use the less informal sentences when speaking to someone you have never met before. In particular, you would only say 'My name is . . . .' when the other person has not met you before.

2 a) quote . . . . . orders
   b) charged . . . . account
   c) invoice
   d) gross . . . . net
   e) overtime

UNIT TEN   The Exhibition

Extensive listening

1 a) There are four public announcements giving information about the catalogues, the Child Playcare Centre, Money Mail and about a lost child.

b) You hear three salesmen. The other people you hear are an organiser of the exhibition and a visitor.

2

lling Points	Salesman A (tin opener)	Salesman B (polish)	Salesman C (water beds)
onomical		✓	
fe	✓		
althy			✓
lti-purpose		✓	
pular			✓

The tin opener is safe. There are no sharp edges. You can't cut yourself.
The polish is economical. You only need to use a little. What you don't use you can put back in the bottle. It is also multi-purpose. You can use it on many different kinds of surfaces.
The water beds are healthy. They are good for you. Chiropractors recommend them. They are also popular. Many people in different countries sleep on them.

Intensive listening

1 a) about   c) the best part of
     b) around   d) in the region of

2 a) *false* – He says he is not usually taken in by salesmen. He is usually very cautious.
     b) *true* – He says they were 'convinced by the demonstration'.
     c) *false* – He emphasises the fact that it was cheap. It was only four pounds – 'so we bought it'.
     d) *false* – He does not say he is angry nor does he sound angry.
     e) *true* – He sounds amused.
     f) *true* – It is useful for 'home decorating' and for 'cutting tiles'. If he puts cork tiles on his kitchen floor it will be useful for that.

3 a) *No* – They should go to the information desk.
     b) *Yes* – Mathew is seven years old and the Playcare centre is for children aged two to nine.
     c) *Yes* – At Money Mail, you can get 'advice about money matters'. This probably includes advice about borrowing money from a bank.
     d) *No* – Catalogues cost one pound forty so she hasn't got enough.

Study point

1 a) iv) emphasising truthfulness
     b) ii) claiming the product is unique
     c) i) being very dramatic
     d) vi) repeating phrases, often in threes
     e) v) quoting scientists or other experts
     f) iii) quoting statistics

2 a) i) drain
     ii) pour
     iii) squeeze . . . . . wring

iv) suck
v) leak
vi) squirt

b) These are some other examples of how these verbs can be used.
I've made the tea. Shall I pour you a cup?
The petrol tank in your car is leaking. It may be dangerous.
They want to drain the land which was flooded last month.
When he cut the orange, some juice squirted in his eye.
The children prefer to suck their drinks through a straw.
When you've washed the towel, please wring it out and hang it up to dry.

c) These are some other verbs associated with liquids.
     spill   strain   soak   seep   drip
Be careful. Don't spill the coffee on your new dress.
When the spaghetti is cooked, please strain it for me.
There are some dirty marks on these towels so I'm going to soak them overnight.
He was cut badly and the blood was seeping through his shirt.
We can't turn the tap off properly. It has been dripping all night.

UNIT ELEVEN   The News

Extensive listening

1 3 UK news
     2 world news
     4 traffic report
     1 foreign correspondent's report

2 a) drugs   political violence
     a fight in a pub   a typhoon
     an international agreement
     a road accident
     b) a typhoon

3 a) *Mrs Beale – worried*
     She was worried that her husband might have been involved in the violence between loyalists and republicans.
     b) *Joseph Doyle – pleased*
     He was pleased because the police had seized a large amount of heroin. It was one of the biggest US drugs seizures in ten years.
     c) *Mr Gilpin – disappointed*
     He was disappointed because India signed an agreement with the Soviet Union not with Britain.
     d) *Mary Hanlon – frustrated*
     She was frustrated because she could not drive south very easily because an accident had caused delays on the road.

Intensive listening

1 a) ii) a person who is hurt accidentally
     b) iii) made more difficult
     c) ii) promises
     d) iii) groups

2 a) ii) The part-time policeman in Northern Ireland was shot at from a car.
  b) i) In Stoke, one man was hurt and one killed.
  c) iii) Mr Williams didn't realise he was growing cannabis.
  d) i) Drivers were told the warning signals were not working.

Study point

1 a)

> The passive is often used in news broadcasts sometimes because we are more interested in what happened than in who or what caused it to happen. This might be because we do not know who or what caused the action e.g. *Bottles and bricks were thrown. Or this might be obvious*, e.g. *Two men were arrested (by the police). Houses were washed away (by the typhoon).*
>   Also, use of the passive with verbs of reporting makes news broadcasts sound more impersonal and more objective, e.g. *His condition is described as stable. It is estimated that a hundred people took part. The agreement is believed to be the first of its kind.* The passive also occurs frequently in scientific texts for similar reasons.

  b) i) Two passenger ferries had been sunk.
     ii) A part-time policeman has been injured.
     iii) He was hit by shots fired from a car.
     iv) Two motor bikes were set on fire.
     v) Drivers are asked to take extra care.

2 a)

Neutral	Strong/dramatic
reach	strike
break out	*erupt*
tear	*rip*
break	*smash*
disrupt	*cripple*

  b) i) The typhoon ripped across central Taiwan yesterday.
     ii) Communications in many areas were crippled.
     iii) Violence erupted in Ulster last night.
     iv) The windows of two pubs and three houses were smashed.

UNIT TWELVE Sing Jazz

Extensive listening

1 to learn more about jazz
  to express themselves through music
  to sing with or for other people
  to earn a living as a singer
  to be as good as possible

2 a) All of these singers want to learn more.
  b) Some of them are ambitious professionally.
  c) None of them think they are perfect singers.
  d) One of them sounds older than the others.
  e) All of them seem to be having a good time.

Intensive listening

1 a) ii) Shirin has decided to work hard at improving her singing.
     She has not been given a job. She has never had any professional experience. She says 'I want to start being a professional now.'
  b) i) Donna and Catherine want to know more about jazz singing.
     Donna says 'I wanted to learn about the jazz styles of singing.' and Shirin says 'I've been singing . . . many different styles, but like Donna, I also wanted to find out about the jazz style.'
  c) iii) All his life, Ken has only had the chance to sing at home until now.
     He says 'I've been a frustrated jazz singer all my life . . . .' and here's the first chance that I . . . get to perform in front of – or not in front of – people.'

2 a) opportunity . . . . . own . . . . individual
  b) creative . . . . . confines

3 When Ken says his voice is not all that marvellous, the others disagree. Donna says 'rubbish' meaning 'that's not true'. Because she is paying him a compliment Ken says, 'You say that to all the boys.' They laugh because Ken is old enough to be her father.

Study point

1

Noun	Adjective	Adverb
flexibility	flexible	flexibly
voice	vocal	*vocally*
rhythm	rhythmic/rhythmical	*rhythmically*
technique	*technical*	technically
expression	expressive	expressively
creativity	*creative*	creatively
emotion	emotional/emotive	emotionally/emotively

Note: 'Rhythmic and rhythmical have the same meaning, but 'emotional' and 'emotive' have different meanings. 'Emotional' means having strong feelings or easily moved and is used to describe people. 'Emotive' is used to describe something which can cause strong feelings. It is often used about language. e.g. 'home' is a more emotive word than 'house'.

2 This is what was actually said although they could have used some of the fillers in different positions. 'Well, I mean, actually' are more often used at the beginning of an utterance. 'You know' can be used at the beginning or after something has been said.
  a) yeah *I mean* the technical side is certainly a challenge and was a big challenge to me to learn the *actual* technique but it was also very good to *actually* put emotion into it.
  b) yeah *well I mean* I haven't got an incredibly good instrument in my voice and not all that marvellous a voice *you know*.

  Students may like to talk about the kind of music they like for a few minutes and practise using 'well, actually, you know, I mean'. Using these words in conversation can sound very natural but using them too often can be annoying for the listener.

UNIT THIRTEEN   On the Agenda

Extensive listening

1 This is the complete agenda.
1 Apologies
2 *Minutes of the meeting of May 20th*
3 *Matters arising*
4 *Next year's programme*
5 *Elections*
6 *Financial matters*
7 *Date of next meeting*
8 AOB

2
a) *false* – She complained that the last meeting was fixed at a bad time as many people were revising for examinations then.
b) *false* – Steve did not.
c) *true*
d) *true* – Item 5: Brian corrected Carol about when the club's rules allow people to make nominations.
e) *false* – They decided it would be in October on the day and time that Meg suggested.
f) *true* – She closed the meeting without asking if there was any other business. However, nobody noticed this – not even Brian.

Intensive listening

1
1 complaint   5 revising
2 missed   6 way
3 fixed   7 jeopardise
4 crazy

2
i)	We must go for . . .	*Knife*	positive
ii)	a very good example of a genre picture	*Butch*	negative
iii)	a good laugh	*Butch*	positive
iv)	You can get that from a video library	*Butch*	negative
v)	foreign, serious, heavy	*Knife*	negative
vi)	nice, light, jokey	*Butch*	positive
vii)	a well-made film	*Butch*	positive
viii)	a good example of film technique	*Butch*	positive

ii) Brian uses the French word *genre* in a negative way here. He is suggesting that the film is only interesting because it is an example of a particular style and has no other interest.
iv) When Meg says *you can get that from a video library* she is suggesting that the Film Club should show films that are not often seen, not films that anyone can see easily.

3
a) second
b) tenth
c) eight
d) six
e) more

Study point

There is more than one possible answer in several cases.
1 a) ask . . . if/whether
Has . . . . else/more

b) enough/comment
seems/sounds
idea/suggestion/point
Absolutely/Definitely/Certainly
c) anyone/anybody
think . . . about
d) disagree
question/matter
thing/point/problem
Point
e) say
put
for . . . . against'

2

> The passive is often used in reporting the minutes of a meeting. This emphasises that decisions have been made by everyone or by a majority of the members, not by individuals. It makes the report sound more objective and more impersonal. (Compare with the use of the passive in news broadcasts, page 89.)

1 were received   2 was attended
3 were read   4 agreed
5 was made   6 was agreed   7 be held
8 was taken   9 was agreed
10 was reminded   11 be made   12 was pointed
13 were proposed   14 seconded
15 was held
16 was decided   17 will be held

UNIT FOURTEEN   The Maniac Mile

Extensive listening

1
a) In the Maniac Mile race you have to run downhill.
b) The Murder Mile is uphill; the Maniac Mile is downhill.
c) The main aim of the serious athletes was to finish in under four minutes.
d) Yes

2
a) true   d) true
b) false   e) false
c) true   f) false

Intensive listening

1
1 extension   4 gradient
2 uphill   5 puffed
3 reversed   6 approximately

2
a) sympathetic   e) unambitious
b) confident   f) joking
c) unsure   g) encouraging
d) realistic   h) pleased

3 a) One of the runners said *you have to loosen the bolts on your head* before you run the race. He means you have to be crazy to do it. These are some other words and expressions which mean mad or crazy: *He has a screw loose. He is not quite right in the head. He is nuts/loony/loopy.*

b) When Chris asks one of the ladies who have come to watch the race 'Why aren't you taking part?' there are several amusing replies from her and her friends. Look at the tapescript again.

Study point

1 a) How did you do?
   b) no idea
   c) Come on
   d) Not a chance
   e) How was it?
   f) haven't a clue
   g) A bit of both.
   h) Here come
   i) I bet

2

a) **Adjective**	**Noun** (A)	**Noun** (P)
sadistic	sadism	*sadist*
masochistic	*masochism*	masochist

b) **Verb**	**Noun** (A)	**Noun** (P)
organise	*organisation*	organiser
originate	*origin*	*originator*
participate	participation	*participant*

UNIT FIFTEEN Acid Rain

Extensive listening

1 Your notes might look something like these.

1 ACID RAIN
   a) term for air pollution (in rain, snow, hail etc.)
   b) damaging to forests, lakes . . . . buildings, human health

2 CHEMICALS INVOLVED
   a) SO_2 from power stations
   b) NO_x from cars + power stations
   c) O_3 secondary pollutant from NO_x + HC in sunlight
   SO_2– 71% from coal burning p. stations in Midlands
      – UK 1st in Europe – 3.7 m tons p.a.
      – problem for Europe & UK
         * Scandinavia etc. angry
         * Wales, Scotland – fish

3 SOLUTIONS
   a) SHORT TERM
      –immediate cuts – p. stations & cars
   b) LONG TERM
      – change way society thinks & reacts
      (30% club – 22 nations decided to cut S emissions by 1993 (Britain not joined) inc. Sw, Norway Can . . . . . . USSR)
         * use less energy – encourage by
         * recycling schemes
         * change transport system (less cars & good public trans.)
2 Individual answers.

Intensive listening

1 a) SO_2 and NO_x are primary pollutants.
   b) SO_2 comes mainly from power stations.
   c) NO_x comes from cars and power stations.
   d) O_3 is a secondary pollutant.
   e) NO_x + HC + sunlight $\rightarrow O_3$

2 a) *true* – 'Britain is Western Europe's largest emitter of sulphur dioxide.'
   b) *false* – Britain's environment is affected as well. In particular, Wales and the west of Scotland.
   c) *false* – They agreed 'to cut their sulphur emissions by thirty percent on 1980 levels by the year 1993.'
   d) *false* – 'what we really want to see is reductions of between 60 and 90 per cent over the next ten years or so'.

3 a) 1 conserve, 2 rationalise, 3 power, 4 bound, 5 environmental, 6 pollution
   b) i) conserve means save
      ii) rationalise means make more sensible and efficient
      iii) bound means certain

Study point

1 a) I'm going to talk about acid rain.
   b) I'm going to talk about exactly what acid rain is and why it's a problem.
   c) Then I'm going to finish off by saying what we can do about it.

      Other ways of beginning a talk are:
      Firstly, I'd like to talk about . . .
      I shall explain exactly . . . . .
      Finally, I want to suggest what . . . . .
   d) Now I'm going to talk about
   e) Now perhaps I should go on to
      Other ways of starting a new section are:
      So now I want to look at . . .
      Okay. Now I'm going to turn to . . .
      Right. Now I'll move on to . . . .
   f) There are really three that we should look at
   g) There are short term solutions and there are long term solutions.

      Other ways of indicating sub-sections to come are:
      There are two examples of this.
      There are advantages and disadvantages.
      There are three main groups.
   h) These are the things we must be looking forward to.
      (He is referring back to the things he has just described.)

      Other ways of ending a section are:
      These are the most important ways we can fight pollution.
      (This summarises what has just been said.)
      Without these changes, there is no hope for the future.
      (This draws a conclusion from what has just been said.)

2 a) damage to forests, lakes (etc.)
   b) ozone – secondary pollutant, (i.e) formed by combination of other prim. pollutants
   c) SO_2 in UK ⊖ pollution in Europe
   d) angry with Brit. govt. ☹ done nothing about the problem
   e) pollution in UK (e.g./viz) Wales and W. Scotland
   f) Britain's SO_2 emission (>) anywhere in W., Europe

NOTES

This item is to be returned on or before
the last d...